Me and My Hittas 6

The Final Testament of a Trap God

A Tranay Adams Novel

Me and My Hittas 6

Copyright © 2016 Tranay Adams. All rights reserved.

Warning: The unauthorized reproduction or distribution of this work is illegal. Criminal copyright infringement, including infringement without monetary gain, is investigated by FBI and is punishable by up to five (5) years in federal prison and a fine of $250,000.

All names, characters, and incidents depicted in this book are products of the author's imagination or are used fictitiously. Any resemblance to actual events, locales, organizations, or persons, living or dead, is entirely coincidental, and beyond the intent of the author and publisher.

No part of this book may be reproduced or transmitted in any form or by any means, electronic or mechanical, including photocopying, recording, or by any information storage and retrieval system, without permission in writing from the publisher.

Me and My Hittas 6 / Tranay Adams-1st ed. © 2016

Kindle Formatting: Renee

Editor: Ghost

Cover Artist: Sunny Giovanni

Publisher: Tranay Adams

Let Me Holla At You!

You probably don't know this, but this is my very first street lit story. I was a big fan of the likes of K'wan, Ca$h and Al Saadiq Banks. Whenever they dropped, I would buy their shit without any hesitation. I was an addict for their work. A nigga would stop everything that he was doing and crack that book open, family. I would become lost in those stories, and before I knew it hours would have been done passed and it would be time for me to go to bed for work the next day. At the time I was working as a special ed teacher's assistant. The checks weren't enough to pay all my bills and shit. Me and my brotha were sharing a small, shitty apartment. It wasn't much but it was ours. It was a roof over our heads and a place to call home.

Anyway, I was just getting by. I wasn't making enough to buy the lil' extra shit that I wanted. Now, by no means am I materialistic, but, shit, what mothafucka doesn't want nice shit sometimes? You Griff me? Hell, I wanna look good and bust a chick or two too. I wanted to feel like the man, even if I wasn't. Anyway, so that I could keep my head above water, I started petty hustling and shit. You know, weed and X-pills.

With my pay check and that combined I was okay. I would go to work in the day and do my thang at night. Then my face would be back in them books. I read a lot; I mean, a hell of a lot. I fell back in love with street lit, so much so that I decided to pen my own tale. I wanted to tell a story about niggaz that grew up on my side of the fence. I wanted you to ride shotgun with me through my hood. The mothafucking Eastside Low Bottoms of South Central, Los Scandalous (Nah, that isn't a typo).

So one day I was at work bored as a bitch, wasn't shit to do so my super was like you can take a break or some shit. I thought to myself I'ma take me a mothafucking break. Problem was, I didn't know what to do. That's when I started thinking about this story that you're currently reading, this series. I had already came up with the characters names inside of my head on my way to work. I was working way in Marina Del Rey, so I had about a good hour to an hour and a half to mull thingz over in my head. So I grabbed the brown paper bag that the food I bought from Tam's burgers was in and started jotting down my characters personalities and how they were all linked. Next, I came up with a plot. Now at the time, everybody and their baby daddy was writing about big time drug dealers and them beefing with other crews. I thought that was the way to go, so yeah, a young nigga followed suit. I guess that was the first time I didn't go outta my way to be original, shame on me, right? Fuck y'all don't judge me. Nah, I'm fucking witchu, family.

Back to the story though, I wrote and wrote and wrote, and before I knew it that brown paper bag was tatted the fuck up. So I opened up the Styrofoam container and started writing in the inside of that and then the outside. I went to Walmart and bought a few note pads and a black gel ink pen. Over the next couple of months I had fucked around and filled up about five of six of those note pads with material. (I still have the pads, but I don't know what the fuck I did with that paper bag and that container). I still have material I haven't used from this story too, mind you. I may use it to write a new story or some shit. I knew I had to put this story down on a document, but the problem was I didn't know how to type so I was pecking them keys with one finger. Over time I learned how to type quite decently though.

Now, I had several titles for this book. Here they are: King of the Bottoms, Respect My Gangsta, Bury Me A G (I used that title for another story), Bow Down to my Gangsta (A title Ca$h gave me but I decided not to use it). For a long time my title was RESPECT MY GANGSTA. My word count for the first book was 95,000 words, it would have been more had I chose to use the material from the note pads.

I went on to write several more installments. I got up to five. Now, this part six that you're about to read is almost entirely from scratch. I took scenes from old books that I've written and added them to this. Once I lost interest in writing this story, I started what I have been told is a classic, THE DEVIL WEARS TIMBS. The Devil was premeditated, I had all of the ideas for it in my head; I just had to execute the story. Anyway, after DEVIL I put out the BURY ME A G series, then the Tyson's Treasure series, then A SOUTH CENTRAL LOVE AFFAIR, which is a standalone novel. Afterwards, Respect my Gangsta started calling my name. I knew I had to go back and finish that series off. I couldn't use the title I wanted though, because a couple of authors had already used it. So a nigga sat back for a minute trying to think of a catchy title and one that would make sense to my story. I figured it's a bunch of mothafuckaz in this story that's down to ride for they homeboy, no matter what. Then boom, it hit me! ME AND MY HITTAS. I decided on this title, and I love it.

Well, this is where my head was at when I was writing this series and what the fuck I was doing when it all came to me back in 2011, crazy, right? You reading some shit from way back when? Now some of you have been with me since THE DEVIL WEARS TIMBS, and I've gained some of you along my journey, either way I appreciate you greatly. Since I have left Lockdown I notice those that have stayed down with Tha Pimp and his exploitations of his pen (his hoe). I also peeped those that stopped fucking with me too. Ain't no love loss, I'ma keep going in for those that appreciate what I bring to the table as a writer. I love y'all niggaz, man, make the kid feel special and shit. I can say some of the most outrageous shit and y'all don't take offense 'cause you know it's all love with me. I don't mean shit by it. I'm just having fun and laughing. I'm sure you all can appreciate that.

Alright, enough of my talking, let's get this show on the mothafuckin' road, you Griff me? Tadowl!

Dedicated to those that got down and stayed down, bulletproof love!

Tranay Adams

Me and My Hittas 6

The Final Testament of a Trap God
The saga's conclusion

Previously

Gouch sat in the driver seat of the Hummer changing the channels on the stereo system. The day had been a long and hard one. He and Pavielle spent the greater part of it dropping off shopping bags of money to the families of G-thang, Voodoo and Dip for their funeral services. Pavielle had spent six hours at the first two houses and was going on his tenth hour at this last stop. Though it was hot as fire that day, Gouch didn't dare to put a rush on Pavielle. He was paying his respects to the families of the men and woman that had died in his honor so it was only right that he was allowed time with them. Besides, Gouch would be all right. The A/C made him feel a lot cooler, like a bottle of champagne sitting in a bucket of ice.

Pavielle snatched open the door and deposited himself into the front passenger seat. He slouched down into the seat and fired up a cigarette. He took a casual pull and unleashed white smoke. Gouch could tell that the situation was eating away at him. The pain was etched all over his face. Not to mention, he was sucking on the end of the cigarette like he was a nigga facing life without parole.

"You, all right?" Gouch asked concerned.

"Hell naw, I'm fucked up." Pavielle admitted, dumping ashes into an ashtray. "I need a drink, and bad than a mothafucka, too."

"You tryna hit The Bar Fly?"

"Nah, I'll sulk later." Pavielle told him. "Let's slide up here to see Sazoo."

"All right."

Gouch resurrected the Hummer and merged into traffic.

Pavielle and Gouch engaged Sazoo at Simpson's family mortuary in Inglewood off of Manchester. At first Pavielle thought they had the wrong address but he checked the slip of paper he'd written it on. The address was indeed the right one. But Pavielle wanted to be especially sure, so he called Sazoo and he told him to come to the entrance. Pavielle knocked on the door and a dark skinned cat in a cheap suit answered the door. The cat stood about 5'7 and looked like a walking corpse. The cat said nothing as he allowed The Hood Brothers inside and locked the doors behind them. He signaled for them to follow him and they fell in line behind him. He led them through a dimly lit corridor and into a room that had coffins scattered everywhere. Pavielle and Gouch peeked inside and saw Sazoo smoking from a long, wooden exotic looking pipe. Pavielle and Gouch could tell from the aroma of the weed that it was Grade A. The cat in the cheap suit knocked on the door and garnered Sazoo's attention.

"Sir," the cat spoke in a deep, baritone that didn't match his appearance. "Your guests have arrived." He then gave a bow and went about his business.

Sazoo exchanged pleasantries with Pavielle and Gouch. He offered them a toke of his pipe. Though Gouch refused, Pavielle chose to indulge. He needed something to make him forget about his worries.

"Careful now, that's some powerful sheet." Sazoo warned Pavielle.

"I know what I'm doing, homeboy. I'm not new to this, I'm true to this." Pavielle held the pipe and lit it at the end with a Bic lighter. He took a couple healthy puffs and expelled white smoke.

"You like?" Sazoo asked.

"Oh, yeah," Pavielle coughed and pounded a fist to his chest. "That shit official."

Sazoo took the time to take a couple of puffs himself before speaking. "All right now, let's get down to business." He smacked and rubbed his hands together, having sat the pipe down on a nearby coffin. He motioned for Pavielle and Gouch to follow him as he headed to a couple of coffins at the back of the room. One by one, Sazoo lifted the lids of the coffins and exposed the kilos inside. Pavielle and Gouch looked between both coffins, nodding their heads. They were happy with what they saw before them.

"Dere you have it, Gentlemen," Sazoo said, "Some of da best cocaine on the market; fifty keys, my neegaz."

"Is this the same shit you let me taste in the park?" Pavielle inquired.

"Yes." Sazoo answered, "Now, the money."

Gouch handed Sazoo a duffle bag. Sazoo sat the duffle bag on a nearby coffin and unzipped it. A smile stretched across his pale, yellow face when he saw all of those big face hundred dollar bills.

"You want us to wait while you count it?"

"No. I'm sure it's all here." Sazoo said, outstretching his hand. "Nice doing business with you…I'm sorry, what was your name again?"

"Pavielle, but you can call me, Booby." He shook Sazoo's hand.

"OK, Booby." Sazoo smiled, boasting all thirty-two teeth like he knew something that Pavielle didn't.

Pavielle narrowed his eyes and tilted his head to the side. At that precise moment, several coffins lids came flying open, one by one.

Boom!

Boom!

Boom!

Boom!

Boom!

Men and Women wearing windbreakers with D.E.A emblazoned across the backs of them shot up in the coffins, drawing their weapons on Pavielle and Gouch.

"Don't move mothafuckaz!" one of them shouted.

Pavielle and Gouch observed their surroundings. Once they came to the conclusion that they were busted, they slowly lifted their hands into the air. One of the D.E.A agents jumped out of his coffin and handcuffed both of the brothers. While he was being handcuffed, Pavielle mad dogged Sazoo with contempt in his eyes.

"Aww, come on now, don't look at me like that." Sazoo said without an accent as he pulled his shield from out of his shirt and let it hang against his chest. "You knew the risks in the game 'fore you joined in it. We're all players, you just so happened to be playing on the wrong team."

Pavielle harped up some phlegm and spat it Sazoo's face. Sazoo smiled and wiped the goo from his face with a handkerchief from his back pocket. Once he'd wiped his face clean, he folded up the handkerchief and tucked it into his back pocket.

"Get these pieces of shit outta here." Sazoo ordered the arresting agent. With that said, Pavielle and Gouch were hurriedly ushered out of the room.

She sat there before him on the stool, holding the telephone to her ear. Her makeup ran as tears cascaded down her face. The pain she was feeling couldn't be denied. The expression on her face portrayed that. Her eyes were bloodshot and her jaw was slacked. She didn't know what to say, nor did she know what to do. What he'd told her had sent her world off course and spiraling out of control. Her life would never be the same, and how could it without the love of her life? At this very moment, she hated herself for falling in love with someone like him, but she hated him more for making her love him.

"Vay, did you hear what I said?"

"Yeah…" she took the time to wipe the tears seeping from her eyes. "I heard what you said, but I'm not leaving you in here to rot."

"Wrong. That's exactly what you're going to do." Pavielle stared her dead in the eyes. "You're going to go on with your life and raise our son, and you're going to tell him all about me. You'll raise him to be a better man than me. You'll show him that these streets are a bitch and once she takes a hold of you, it's hard to shake her loose. You tell him how this lifestyle is addictive and you can become hooked on it, like you can any other drug. Whether it be cocaine, heroin, or whatever...the game is a drug. It provides a high and a thrill just like any other narcotic, and there ain't no rehabilitation for the shit."

"I'm going to do all of that, but I'm not just gonna leave you in here." Vayda said defiantly. "You hear me, Pavy? You're going to be outside of these walls to help me raise this beautiful baby of ours, do you understand?"

For a time Pavielle didn't respond, but then he nodded.

"I need to hear you say it, baby."

"I understand."

"Good. I'm coming back to get chu. You just be ready when I get here." She told him. "Alright?"

"I got chu."

Vayda placed her hand flat on the Plexiglas and said, "One life."

From the other side of the Plexiglas, Pavielle placed his hand flat over hers and replied, "One love."

They hung up the telephones at the exact same time. Vayda then rose to her feet and placed a loving kiss on the Plexiglas, leaving a purple imprint behind. 'I love you' she mouthed and then he mouthed it back. They then went their separate ways.

Pavielle walked past Gouch on his way to the door that he'd came in through. They exchanged nods and Gouch went back to the conversation at hand.

"Yeah, Blood, old boy was a D.E.A agent." Gouch shook his head. "Agent Leonard Dukes, mothafucka sunk the whole family."

"Damn." Killa Dre said, hating to hear that.

"Booby talking about holding the weight," Gouch informed him. "He's gonna try to work a deal for me to walk and him to be left holding the bag. Ain't no way in hell I'm letting him do that. And I'm not letting him rot in this bitch, either."

"What chu gone do, my nigga?"

"What chu think?" Gouch gave him a hard, unflinching look. Killa Dre didn't like the look his big homie was giving him. He had a pretty good idea what he was getting at but he hoped that he was wrong.

"Alright, times up!" A C.O came to stand behind Gouch.

"I'm out this bitch, Killa," Gouch said. "Twenty Gang…"

"…Or don't bang." Killa Dre finished the phrase.

They hung up the telephones and made their departure.

$$$

Banga sat behind the wheel of the Dodge Charger nodding his head and drumming his fingers on the steering wheel as he listened to Rick Ross's *Mastermind* CD. He had been waiting on Killa Dre to return from walking Vayda and Little Nasheed to the house in Compton they were going to hole up for the time being. About fifteen minutes later, Killa Dre came strolling to the car. He snatched open the door and planted his ass into the front passenger seat. As soon as Banga rolled out into traffic, he lit up the half of the L he'd been smoking on their way to the county jail. Banga stole a glance in his direction and knew that something was weighing heavily on his mind.

"What's popping, Bleed? You've been tight lipped since we left the tombs."

"Something Gucci said back in county. Well, he didn't actually say it; it was more like a look he gave me."

"What chu mean? What were y'all talking about?"

"He and Booby being locked away inside of The Beast for the rest of their lives," Killa Dre answered. "He wore the look of a man willing to do anything he could to set them free."

"So, what, you think he may rat to save their asses?"

"No. I think he may rat to save his brother's."

Banga laughed his ass off then shot a look at Killa Dre. "Gucci? Snitch? Get the fuck outta here! That nigga's the G'est of the G'est. I don't know about your big homie, but my big homie stand up. My nigga much rather dip his prick in a pond filled with piranhas than roll over. If there's any nigga I'm sure of it's that nigga there."

Killa Dre blew white smoke from the side of his mouth and passed the L to Banga.

"I'm glad you're so sure, homeboy, 'cause I'm not. I've dropped some bodies with that man; I can't gamble on his loyalty." Killa Dre admitted. "For as much as these niggaz out here pop that gangsta shit there's only a handful of 'em that are going to wear that time, feel me?"

"True dat," Banga nodded.

"Pull over at the lil' store right here." Killa Dre directed with his finger.

Banga pulled into the parking lot of a liquor store/ mini mart. Killa Dre fished around inside of the change holder until he gathered up enough coins to make a phone call. After wards, he hopped out of the car and made a beeline to an old raggedy telephone booth that looked like it didn't function. He snatched up the receiver and wiped it off on his shirt and cradled the telephone to his ear. Once he dropped the coins into the slot. He glanced over his shoulder as the line rang.

"What that shit two, B-Man?" Killa Dre spoke into the telephone. "Ain't shit. A nigga straight like six o'clock; listen, are your people still up in county?"

$$$

Gouch sat on the bottom bunk shuffling a deck of playing cards in unique ways as he watched Pavielle brush his hair back into a ponytail.

"What're you getting all snazzy for? We're in a house full of dicks." Gouch stated. "What, you found a nigga you like in here?"

Gouch laughed.

"Nah, I'm going to see the warden." Pavielle said seriously, washing his face in the sink. This wiped the smile off

Gouch's face. He stopped shuffling the playing cards and brought his legs over the bed, allowing his feet to touch the floor.

"For what?"

"You know what for, big bro. We've already discussed this."

"Booby, how long have I had your back?" Gouch asked.

"Since the day mom's pushed me outta her womb."

"Right," Gouch agreed. "So what makes you think that I'ma let chu bite the bullet? The big brother looks out for the little brother. That's how it has always been since the dawn of men."

"I know you've always had my back and I love you for it." Pavielle confessed. "And right now I'm about to prove it by brokering this deal. If this goes my way you'll walk out of here a free man and you'll help Vayda raise your nephew."

"I can't rock with that." He shook his head.

"Well, that's too bad. You may not like it now but just as soon as your ass is on the other side of these walls you'll learn to live with it. Then you'll be thanking me."

"Listen, man…"

Pavielle whipped around, cutting Gouch short, "Nah, you listen, Gregory, for as long as I can remember you've been pulling my ass out of the fire. Now it's time I pulled out yours. You're gonna shut the fuck up and let me do what needs to be done! Or we can get it from the shoulders right now! The loser will be the one left holding the bag!"

"I don't wanna fight chu, baby bro," Gouch raised his hands in surrender, "If this is the way you want it then you got it."

"All right then." Pavielle turned back around to the mirror, checking his teeth for food particles. He was none the wiser to what happened next; Gouch locked his arms around his neck in a Sleeper Hold. Pavielle clenched his teeth and tried to thwart him off but his strength was quickly depleting. He could feel himself weakening and growing sluggish.

"Goddamn you, Gucci, don't chu do this shit to me!"

"I do what I do 'cause I love you."

Pavielle squirmed under Gouch's arms for another three minutes before he was out cold. Gouch placed him into the bottom bunk and covered him with the thin blanket. He then kissed him on the side of the head and approached the door, pounded on it with his fist.

"Yo, C.O!"

A tall, flabby body correctional officer took his time walking down to Pavielle and Gouch's cell.

"What is it this time, Hood?" he asked, as if Gouch was bothering him.

Gouch pulled a crisp folded $100 dollar bill from out of his sock and slid it underneath the door. The C.O examined the bill, making sure it was authentic as he listened to Gouch.

"I need to see the warden."

"About what?"

Gouch looked around as if to see if anyone was listening before replying, "I know about a couple of murders."

The C.O nodded and hurriedly unlocked the cell's door.

$$$

Gouch strode down the tier wearing a smile across his face, which was odd considering he would spend the rest of his natural life behind brick walls and barbwire fences. In spite of his circumstances he found comfort in knowing that his baby brother would be a free man soon. Gouch made a deal with the D.A. He confessed to over fifteen unsolved murders that he'd committed. These were murders that he'd carried out by himself. He didn't mention any of the ones he'd done with anyone else. There wasn't any way he was wearing a *snitch jacket.* His bloodline didn't rock like that. He was a thorough bred, a nigga of a far greater pedigree. He wasn't going to suck anyone into his bullshit. If he was going to go down then he was going to go down by himself. Gouch knew that Pavielle would hate him for what he had done, but he was sure that he would forgive him after a while. Once Pavielle had Little Nasheed in his arms and Vayda by his side he'd realize what he had done was for the greater good.

Gouch had just approached his cell's door when four Mexicans emerged from the cell next to it. They all wore hard faces and gripped shanks the size of Butcher knives. Gouch looked to his rear and four more Mexicans were coming up the tier, they were carrying shanks as well.

$$$

Pavielle slowly stirred awake from the educed sleep Gouch had put on him. He sat up in bed and peeled open his eyes. He looked around groggily and then it dawned on him what had occurred. "Shit." He scrambled to his feet and ran over to the door of his cell. He pounded on it as hard as he could and called for the C.O. He stopped once he saw Gouch approaching, but knew something was wrong from the expression on his face. That's when he saw the Mexicans closing in on him. Pavielle knew that some shit was about to crack off.

He figured that the best he could do was make enough noise to get the C.O's attention. With that thought it mind, Pavielle pounded and kicked the door with all of his might. His attack on the door grew louder and louder seeing the Mexican's stabbing Gouch up. Tears escaped his eyes and he felt his heart crumbling, but he ushered on, assaulting the door unmercifully. He hoped and prayed that someone would come and rescue his brother.

$$$

The Mexicans rushed Gouch from both sides, attacking from all angles with the shanks. Gouch tried to put up a fight but his efforts proved futile. The shanks hit him from every direction you could think of and even after he'd grown limp, they kept on coming. Grunts and vulgarities escaped the lips of the Mexicans as they plunged the blades deep into Gouch's body. The sound of metal hitting flesh filled the air and specks of blood clung to the walls and dripped thick upon the floor. Once the Mexicans were done butchering Gouch, they hoisted him up, and threw him over the railing, American Me style.

"Guuuuucccci," Pavielle's screamed ripped through the air. Tears poured down his face in buckets seeing what had been done to his brother. He saw the Mexicans leaning over the railing peering down at Gouch. Once they saw that he was dead they turned and walked away. The alarm for lockdown blared loud and furiously. Pavielle took a good look at the faces of the men involved in Gouch's murder. He branded their descriptions into the walls of his memory. Come hell or high water, he would get his revenge even if it meant his undoing.

"You're dead, you hear me? Every last one of you bitches are dead, count on it!" Pavielle breathed fire. Spittle flew from his lips and his hot breath fogged up the rectangle shaped window of his cell's door. He placed his back against the wall and slid down to the floor. Placing his face into the palms of his hands, he cried long and hard.

A Tranay Adams Novel

Chapter One

Pavielle stood under the spray of the hot water inside of the prison's shower room. He lathered himself up with a bar of soap, masking his body white. Sitting the bar of soap down on the wet tiled floor, he picked up a small bottle of shampoo & conditioner and squeezed some of it into the palm of his hand. Once he sat the bottle down, he went on to massage the gel into his scalp. Afterwards, he planted his hands on the wall and bowed his head, shutting his eyelids. He took a deep breath as the hot liquid beat down upon him and washed over his skinny body. He swiped the water from out of his face and allowed the showerhead's water to keep rinsing him. The soap that was rinsed from off his form went swirling down the drain.

Many things were going through Pavielle's mind at the moment, but the main one that he was focused on was his older brother, Gouch. No matter how hard he tried he couldn't escape the horrifying images that assaulted his mental on nightly bases. He couldn't help seeing the movie of his sibling's demise every night when he laid down and shut his eyelids. All he could see was the Mexicans rushing his brother and grunting as they plunged shanks in and out of his body hatefully. Then there was Gouch's face of pain and his howls as he was brutally attacked. The last thing he saw was the Vatos lifting him up and throwing him over the guard railing. Pavielle broke down sobbing as soon as he heard Gouch's form impact the floor below. He knew then that without the shadow of a doubt that his brother was dead.

Before Gouch had been killed, he managed to broker a deal that granted Pavielle his freedom. The next day the warden had came to see him with a couple of documents and telling him that he'd be a free man in a few days. Amongst the sensitive information on the documents were several murders that Gouch had confessed to committing. When Gouch took full responsibility for the murders, he freed several of the homies up from doing time that were still on the streets, as well as those that were already locked up doing time. With this move niggaz from the hood never had to worry about getting the charges because Gouch had taken them for them. This was a selfless act that many homies would be grateful for. Gouch had gone out like the gangsta the streets knew him to be.

Flashback

The day was bright and warm thanks to the glowing marble that was the sun. Its rays shined on Gouch's sweaty body as he practiced martial arts moves upon the brick wall in the backyard. His perspiring form glistened like a palm full of diamonds under the sun. You could tell that the young man was really into the Ninjitsu style of fighting; because he was so into his training he'd forgotten he had an audience.

"What is he doing?" Panic asked Pavielle, stuffing his face with Fiddle Faddle. Panic was a kid too big for his age. He had a complex about his size. And had no quarrels with putting hands on anyone that made fun of him. His pie shaped face and round about body gave him the appearance of a snowman.

"Ninjitsu," Pavielle answered, sticking his hand into the box of the sweet caramel coated popcorn. Pavielle was a skinny brown-skinned kid with thick hair that he wore pulled back in a fluffy puff. He had a quick temperament and even quicker fists. Though he was only twelve years old, he carried himself with the swagger of a seasoned gangster. He was like the live and in the flesh version of Riley Freeman from The Boondocks cartoon.

"Gazuntite." Panic thought his friend had sneezed.

Pavielle laughed. "Nah, my nigga, Ninjitsu is a style of fighting. You know, like Karate or Judo?"

"Oh." Panic shrugged and continued to feed his face.

"We've gotta problem, blood." A voice came from beneath the boys from where they sat. They turned around and found Debo and Rydah Man. The boys looked like they'd been in the fight of their lives. Their clothing was smeared with blood and dirt, rips and tears covering them. Debo had a black eye and a busted lip while Rydah Man wore a bloody nose and lumps on his forehead.

Pavielle and Panic jumped down from where they were sitting.

"Damn, blood, what the fuck happened to y'all?" Panic asked. Caramel popcorn residue was stuck around his mouth and cheeks.

Gucci!" Pavielle yelled over his shoulder to his brother.

Gouch jumped down from off the wall, pulling his wife-beater back over his head. "What's bracking?" he asked, with a serious look, taking in the sight of his two homeboys.

"Mexicans G'd us for the courts at Trinity." Rydah Man informed him.

"Nigga busted my ball with his knife, too." Debo said, holding up his deflated Spalding before smacking it down on the pavement.

"How many?" A scowling Gouch asked.

"Eight. But chu know me and Rydah down for ours, blood. We tried to squabble with them, but what could we do? They were grown men and we're lil' niggaz."

"Booby, get unc's strap from outta the house and don't let momma see you getting it."Gouch told him. While Pavielle was gone Rydah Man and Debo filled Gouch in on exactly what happened at the park between them and the Mexicans.

"That shit gone." Pavielle told Gouch as he approached him. "He either moved it or took it with him."

"Damn," Gouch said. "You check in his bedroom under the mattress and in the cabinet above the stove?"

"Yep."

"Fuck it." Debo stated. "I'm about to call my brother."

"Nah, Dee." Gouch stopped him. "We can't go running to get our relatives every time a beef pops off. We've gotta handle shit ourselves. It's the only way we'll ever get our respect."

"My brother is right, blood." Pavielle chimed in.

"I ain't letting this shit ride, Gucci. Niggaz violated so they gotta pay. And I want my reparations in pints of blood, ya Griff me?" Debo said firmly.

"Two sho," Gouch replied. "This is the set and we gone hold it down."

"So what the fuck we gone do then?" Debo asked, getting frustrated. He was ready to make a move.

"What chu think we gone do, Outlaw?" Gouch inquired. "We're gone strap up and bring it to these pussies."

"Strap up?" Panic frowned. "How are we gone do that? You said Gangsta's gun is gone."

"You don't have to have guns to be strapped up, Panic." Gouch told him as he gave the backyard the once over. He hurriedly picked up the items that would do the most damaged to flesh and bone. He gave Pavielle a rusty chain with a padlock at the end of it, Panic a baseball bat, Debo a busted water-pipe and Rydah Man a crowbar. Gouch gave his homies the once over. They were all packing.

"Now y'all strapped." He told them.

"You aren't tooling up?"

"Nah, Debo." Gouch began. "All I need are these." He held up his fists. "Now, let's show these chumps what time it is."

The youths gave a loud Hoorah, throwing their weapons in the air. Gouch motioned for them to follow him and they fell in line behind him as he headed out of the backyard.

The youths mobbed up Adams with Gouch stalking ahead of them. Gouch wasn't exactly the leader type, but being the oldest out of the crew made him the leader by default. The boys often looked to him when they had a conflict on their hands.

When the boys made it to Trinity Park the Vatos were still on the outside courts playing basketball without a care in the world. Gouch knew a few of them by face and reputation, but the others were alien to him. Gouch called Rydah Man to his side and threw his arm over his shoulder.

"Which one of these fools were the ones that busted your ball?" he asked.

"That one right there, in the Carolina blue basketball shorts." Rydah Man pointed him out.

Gouch followed Rydah Man's finger to a Spanish kid about 19 years old. He was laughing and jogging up the court after making a three point jump shot. He had a thin mustache and a shaved-head. Tattooed on the back of his head was a sexy lady with her legs wide open to her hairy vagina.

"Alright, fallback," Gouch patted Rydah Man on the back before starting in tattoo-head's direction. He had just stolen the ball and was headed his way, bouncing it. Gouch tripped him and he crashed to the pavement, busting his mouth. *Tattoo-head grimaced and pulled his switchblade from his waistband, flicking it open. His homeboys watched as he rose to his feet and turned his blade on Gouch.*

Tattoo-head spat blood and wiped his mouth with the back of his hand. "You're dead, mayate."

Tattoo-head lunged to stab Gouch and he grabbed him by the wrist, twisting it and causing him to drop his switchblade. Still clutching tattoo-head's wrist, Gouch whipped around, bringing the heel of his sneaker across his jaw with all of his might. The blow sent a spray of blood and broken teeth into the air. Tattoo-head hit the pavement with his eyes rolled to the back of his skull.

Seeing their comrade bite the dust, tattoo-head's homeboys started in on Gouch. Panic leapt into action swinging his baseball bat with all of his weight behind it. The bat connected with one of the Vato's arms making a sickening sound that mimicked a chicken bone breaking in half. The Vato let out a howl of pain and his face twisted in agony. Pavielle came right behind Panic, striking his adversary across the head and splitting his wig. The man let go of a blood curdling scream and grabbed for the wound as it spilled blood. Pavielle continued to thrash him with his rusted chain, as he lay in shock. Next was Debo, he brought his busted pipe across a Vato's kneecap. When the man went to clutch his aching knee, Debo swung his pipe like a golf club, laying him at his feet. The boys were delivering a one sided beating to the Vatos. Their enemies were at the mercy of the weapons they'd chosen to bear arms with.

After dropping one of the Vatos with a roundhouse kick across the jaw, Gouch took time to admire his homeboys' handiwork. Unbeknownst to him, one of the Vatos had snuck away to his jeans which lie under the shade of a tree. He fished around in the pocket of the jeans until he produced a .38 revolver. He drew a bead on Pavielle who was beating one of his homies with his chain, and as he applied pressure to the trigger, a pigeon latched onto him and pecked him in the eye. He shrieked and fired a wild shot that froze everyone in their tracks. Everyone looked on as another pigeon came, then another, and then another until the gunman's upper body was covered with pigeons. The gunman spun around wildly, screaming and firing shots blindly. He tripped and fell on his back, where the pigeons continued to devour his hide. Everyone watched in horror, not a soul present had seen such a sight.

"Coo. Coo. Coo." A voice mimicked the pigeons' native tongue. Everyone looked over their shoulders and found a tall, slender brother in a worn brown leather duster in the distance. The pigeons flew away from the gunman, leaving behind a mangled mutilated corpse with hollow eye-sockets. Feathers floated in the air as the pigeons flapped their way over to their keeper. Some of the pigeons littered their keeper's head and shoulders while others returned to the power lines just above his head. The keeper winked at Pavielle and walked away, his leather duster brushing over the ground.

"The Birdman," Pavielle uttered in awe.

"Come on y'all; let's get the fuck outta here." Gouch yelled and waved his homies on as he ran out of the park. The boys were right on his heels.

Present

Pavielle took off his towel and left himself nude for a time as he got dressed in his underwear. Standing on the side of him was a correctional officer by the name of, Fuller. He was a stocky, light skinned brother with tattooed arms. He wore glasses that he pushed upon his nose every so often being that they were too big. But this still didn't prompt him to purchase himself another pair. Fuller was an ex-street nigga always looking to make a few extra bucks to ensure that his family of five wanted for nothing.

At the time Fuller was chewing gum and pushing his glasses back upon his nose, watching the entrance of the shower room as he and Pavielle chopped it up.

"So, you know who these fools are that made that move on my brother?" Pavielle pulled his boxer briefs upon his waist and grabbed his wife beater.

"Unh huh," he chewed on his gum. "I know exactly who they are; I saw all of their faces when they made the move."

"You sure you can get your hands on the information that I asked for?"

"Oh, most def." he replied, still watching the entrance. "Long as that paypa is straight, I'll have it for you."

"I may need you to make something else happen for me. It may be a tall order but I'll make it worth your while."

"Whatever you need."

"Bool," He laced up his sneakers.

"Question?"

"Shoot."

"If the government ceased all your assets and froze your accounts. Just how in the hell do you plan on funding this lil' scheme of yours?"

"Fuller."

"'Sup?"

"Anybody ever tell you youz a nosey mothafucka?"

"My bad, dawg."

"None of that is any of your concern, long as you get paid."

"You mothafucking right."

Pavielle slipped his shirt over his head and smacked the door of his locker shut.

"Let's go, freedom waits."

***

Warden Danz made his way down the hallway headed in Pavielle and Fuller's direction. He was a stocky man with a shaggy, salt and pepper beard. He had thick bags under his eyes and thin pink lips. He had a balding scalp, but long hair on the sides which he wore pulled back in a ponytail. Danz winced as he moved down the corridor with a limp, his cane assisting him along the way. The sixty eight year old man was dressed in a cheap blue suit and pattern leather shoes. The three men stopped when they reached each other inside of the hall.

"Fuller," Danz gave him a nod in greeting.

"Sir." the correctional officer replied, returning the nod. He frowned having noticed him limping with the cane. "Are you, okay?"

"Oh, yes, I'm fine." he answered, wincing. "I'm still in pain from a recent car accident."

A car accident? This nigga was moving down the hall like he got ass raped or some shit, Pavielle thought as he took a good look at the warden.

"Alright, I hope you feel betta." Fuller told him.

"Thanks for your concern." Danz turned his eyes on Pavielle. "Mr. Hood, I see you're on your way home."

Pavielle blew hard and angled his head, folding his arms across his chest. He scowled at the warden and twisted his lips. He wasn't trying to hear shit that mothafucka had to say.

"Yep," Pavielle replied with a fucked up attitude.

"It's rare in life that we get a second chance, I hope you make the best of yours." Danz extended his wrinkled, liver spotted hand. "Good luck, son."

Pavielle looked down at his hand like he'd just wiped his ass with it. When he looked back up in his eyes he twisted his lips like *Fuck up out of here with that bullshit.*

"Check this out, I'ma free man now and you're cutting into my time," Pavielle began. "I got places to go and people to see."

Fuller looked at him like he was crazy. Although he didn't know why in the hell he was surprised. The young kingpin had been popping fly shit since he was handed his jailhouse uniform and necessities. The nigga was more arrogant and prideful than anyone he had ever met. He had to salute his G though, because he was gangsta no matter where his ass was at.

"You're right, you're a free man now," Danz said. "I just want you to…"

Pavielle kept on walking, letting the warden's word hit his back. He didn't have any words for dude.

Fuller looked at Danz and shrugged. He then jogged ahead to catch up with Pavielle.

"Hey, homie, you ain't have to come at the old man like that," he told the young kingpin. "That nigga Danz ain't that bad."

"Fuck Danz, fuck this jail, fuck these cons, fuck these guards and fuck the system." Pavielle said, moving down the corridor past an inmate that was mopping the floor. His eyes were focused ahead. "I don't care about nothing but bringing my brotha's killers to justice, street justice, homeboy."

Fuller looked around nervously trying to make sure that no one had overheard him. He got right beside Pavielle and spoke in a hush tone in his ear.

"I'ma help you get these niggaz, but chu gotta keep it low key, fam. We don't won't niggaz to know what's finna go down and botch these hits, you feel me?'

"I got chu, homeboy. You just make sure you handle that business that we discussed."

"I got that, you ain't even gotta worry about it."

"Good to know." he continued his stride, still staring ahead.

Chapter Two

The gate buzzed and Pavielle came strolling out, a wrinkled brown paper bag of his belongings in his vein riddled hand. He was wearing the same shit he was when he first walked through The Gates of Hell, and it all was wrinkled. From the look on his face you could tell that he didn't give a fuck. Nah, this nigga had other shit on his mind. So his appearance was the least of his concerns. Pavielle had black bags under his eyes and his eyes were red webbed. A five o'clock shadow was on the lower half of his face. He didn't need a drink. Not at all, he needed several drinks, and a blunt of some of the most potent weed known to men.

The young kingpin never broke his stride as he made his way towards the black on black Cadillac Escalade truck waiting on him. The sun shined before his eyes, causing his eyelids to narrow. Hunching his head slightly, he kept it moving until he reached the front passenger side door. Opening the door, he hopped into the front passenger seat and slammed the door shut behind him. Slumping down in his seat, he fished out the half smoked blunt from out of the ash tray and sparked it up, expelling smoke from his nostrils.

"'Sup, blood?" Someone spoke from the backseat.

Pavielle flipped down the sun-visor and looked through the rectangle shaped mirror. Making eye contact with Banga, he threw his head back in greeting.

"'Sup with it, my young nigga?" He said like he was exhausted. Banga's forehead slightly creased as he stared at Pavielle. The nigga looked like he had slept in the dumpster wearing those clothes and climbed out of it once he heard that they were there to pick him up. He already knew why he looked like he had been through hell and back. Although he had lost his little brother, Playboy, in the beef between them and Nightmare's people, his big homie had lost his uncle, brother, grandmother and countless homies. He could only imagine what he was feeling right then. He knew right then that what they say was indeed true "Heavy is the head that wears the crown." Being Top Dawg was a headache, which was exactly why Banga didn't want that spot. He'd much rather play his position as soldier. It didn't bother him that he was just another pawn on the chessboard.

"Ain't 'bout shit, big homie. You know a Y.G just out here holding it down, ya feel me?" Banga replied.

"Two sho'." he nodded his understanding. "How you doing though, fam? I mean, since bro bro's passing and all."

"Maintaining, tryna keep it together. You know how it is. I should be asking you the same though."

"I'm fucked up. I mean, a nigga really, really fucked up out here," Pavielle admitted. "I'm just gone roll with the punches and deal with it. That's all a nigga can do, you Griff me? We signed up for this shit. So we know all that comes with it. We've smoked niggaz family and they smoked ours. You do dirt you get dirt. Can't start crying when it's yo' turn."

"True dat," Banga focused his attention out of the window.

"So what's up, blood? How we moving now that you back on the turf?" Killa Dre asked Pavielle.

Killa Dre had called off the hittas he had on standby at the county Jail. At first, he thought that B-Man's people had made that hit on Gouch. But when he got word back that they didn't carry it out, he was relieved and confused. Relieved because he avoided making a huge mistake and confused because he couldn't put his finger on who exactly ordered Gouch's murder.

"I'm out." Pavielle responded like it was just as simple as that.

Killa Dre's face balled up as he looked to his big homie. "What chu mean you're out? You walking away from all of what you built? Shit, what we've built? Niggaz are depending on you to eat out here. You just can't up and leave."

"I know that, and I'm not going to." he assured him. "I did some thinking since I was in that fucking cage, and this is what I've come up with. I'ma let chu take over."

"Me?" Killa Dre raised an eyebrow.

"Yeah, unless these shoes ain't your size."

"Oh, nah. They're definitely my size. I'm just surprised. I wasn't expecting it to be so soon."

"Well, me either, but here we are. So I hope you're ready."

"Shiiiet, a young nigga stay ready."

"Good." Pavielle said. "Like I was saying, I'ma plug you in with the connect. I'ma put the love on these fools that peeled bro bro and then I'm getting the fuck outta the way."

"Sounds like a plan." Banga spoke from the backseat.

"No doubt," Killa Dre added, looking through the windshield.

"Where's Vayda and my son holed up at?" Pavielle inquired.

"They're safe," Banga told him. "They at my people's house in Compton, they're hold 'em down out there. They'll be all right."

"Bool."

"Oh, I almost forgot." Killa Dre said, snapping his fingers recalling something.

"What's up?" Pavielle's forehead crinkled and he threw his head back slightly. "Black Jesus wants to see you. He wanted me to see about getting you to come by to see him." he informed him. "I told 'em that I'd tell you, but knowing you you'd say 'fuck him.'" he looked at him to confirm what he felt he would say.

Pavielle seemed to be thinking on it for a time, massaging his chin. "Nah, you can slide me up there to homie's place."

"What?" Killa Dre looked at him surprised.

"You heard right, youngin, we riding out up there to see what's popping." He told him. "First, I need you to take me somewhere."

"Where?"

"I'll tell you. It's all up here," he tapped his finger to his temple. "Make this right at the corner here." He gave the directions and Killa Dre obliged.

Flashback

"You think unc rushing us home for that shit at the park?" Pavielle asked Gouch as he lit up a blunt. He took a pull and held the smoke in his lungs for a time before blowing it in the air.

"Shit, I don't know," Gouch shrugged, "Probably so."

"You think it has anything to do with me striking up the hood in that alley behind the house?"

Gouch looked at Pavielle like he was the dumbest mothafucka in the world. "Nigga, I know you didn't. You know how that nigga is! He don't won't us tagging nowhere around the house! You saw how he tripped the first time he caught us; my mothafucking chest still sore. You don't know how to strike the hood up anyway. You think he don't know your chicken scratch?"

"Blood, fuck all that!" Pavielle twisted up his face and waved him off. "This is our mothafucking hood, and niggaz gotta know so when they roll through!"

"I Griff you," Gouch nodded. "But I'm not tryna hear this man's mouth. You know how he be going in about this and that. All that's gone do is piss him off. You know he don't want us pushing the set."

"Shit, I don't see why not! He's pushing it, why can't we?"

"He doesn't want us making the same mistakes as he did in life." Gouch told him.

Pavielle laughed. "It's a lil' too late for that shit, buddy. We right in the heart of the mothafucking 20s! It ain't shit to do but bang duce-owe and beef with the crabs. Hell, it ain't like he's done a good job of sheltering us from this shit anyway," Pavielle took another pull of his blunt before passing it to his brother. He expelled the smoke and continued. *"He should be flattered. I don't wanna be a doctor or binem. I wanna be like my uncle Gangsta, from Eastside 20s."* he stated proudly.

"Me too," Gouch blew smoke into the air and passed the blunt back to his sibling. "I feel the same way." He spat on the ground. "He won't us to change, then he's gotta change too, and set a mothafucking example. 'Cause I don't see no other way. This gangbanging shit is me."

"Shit," Pavielle's face lit up with surprise.

"What up?" Gouch asked concerned.

"Gangsta," he nodded to a husky man in a Chicago Bulls jersey and matching fitted cap. He was standing on the front porch of a white and gray two-story house. Pavielle threw down what was left of the blunt and mashed it into the sidewalk, smearing black ash. He took a bottle of knock-off

Versace cologne from his pocket and sprayed himself down. He handed the bottle over to his brother who proceeded to do the same.

After handing the bottle back to him, Gouch reached into his pocket and produced a pack of Winter Fresh gum. He withdrew two sticks of gum; one for himself and the other for his sibling. The two popped the gum into their mouths and chewed as they approached their grandmother's home. The boys knew their uncle would get in their asses if they came back home smelling like they'd bathed in a tub of marijuana. Gangsta could care less if his nephews got high, he just didn't want to hear his mother's mouth about it.

Gouch and Pavielle came through the iron-gate of their grandparents' home. Their uncle stood at the edge of the porch glaring at them. Swallowing the golf ball sized lumps in their throats, they moved forward. They had no idea what they had done but they braced themselves for the worse outcome. If they were lucky it would just be a scolding or a hard punch to the chest. If not, it would be a head up fade with their uncle.

The boys stopped at the bottom of the steps. As their uncle descended upon them, they bowed their heads in submission. Gangsta looked as if he was about to snarl and attack his nephews as if he were a savaged beast.

Gangsta was a man large in size and reputation. He was the O.G shot-caller of the Eastside Outlaw Rolling 20s Bloods Gang. Though his gun went off, he was more about his paper than anything else. He was the neighborhood dopeman and was quickly rising to kingpin status.

Gangsta stopped at the last step, looking from Gouch to Pavielle. Rustling up enough courage, Gouch managed to look his uncle in his eyes. He tried to match his glare but he failed miserably.

"What's up, unc?" Gouch asked flatly. Gangsta didn't bother to answer his oldest nephew; he set his sights on his youngest instead.

"Aye," Gangsta addressed Pavielle, snapping his fingers for his attention. "What I tell you about looking a man in his eyes when he's talking to you?"

Pavielle looked into the eyes of the man who had been more father than uncle to him and spoke, "What's up with it, unc?"

"Ya'll two niggaz! That's what's up!" Gangsta mad dogged them. "Word is, y'all been out here tearing shit up, getting into all kinds of bullshit."

"Nah, it ain't like that, unc," Gouch said. "We haven't even been…" he was cut short by a dirty look from Gangsta.

"Now, I done told y'all asses what the deal is in these streets, gangbanging ain't no joke. It ain't for lil' boys. This is grown man business. The crips, the bloods, the eses; they're all playing for keeps; they don't give a rats ass if y'all are just kids. If you outta bounds and an enemy catches you slipping, that's it!" He made his hand into the shape of a gun and pointed it at each of his nephews' foreheads, saying Blam! "The niggaz in this life don't give a mad ass fuck, you Griff me?" Pavielle and Gouch nodded yes. "So, if you're ready to get your officials; bang duce-owe, carry a strap all day every day, and grow eyes in the back of your head. And live life as a paranoid, itchy trigger-finger mothafucka, then be my guest," He paused before continuing. "But heed my warning my young nephews, with this here…" Gangsta showed his nephews the ink on his forearm. Tattooed there was a burning skull with two long-nose .44 revolvers on either side of it, and on its forehead was Eastside R.T.B.G 26th street clique; C.K Mafia. "Comes with three things for certain," Gangsta continued. "The hospital, the pen and the graveyard; you'll see the first two if you're lucky. If not, all of them. I've been to two of them already. Take it from me; y'all don't wanna get started up in this bullshit, man. If I could, that's on my daddy I'd take it all back and have my ass on somebody's football field somewhere." Pavielle noticed the nasty scar on his uncle's neck he had gotten from an ice-pick like shank during a prison riot. He was only five years old then. Then he remembered the month long stay in county general he endured after some Mexicans sprayed his car. It was a miracle that Gangsta had survived. A bullet ricocheted off his skull, another one had gone in and out of his bicep, and he still had one lodged in his chest.

"Make no mistake about what y'all are tryna get into," Gangsta continued. "The 20s are like the mob...once you get in you can't get out. The ball is in your court. It's all on y'all." he looked to his nephews waiting for their replies. He hoped that he'd gotten through to them.

The boys answer was yes even after hearing their uncle's big speech, but they decided to make it seem as if they were debating their decision before answering. They didn't want Gangsta to think what he said went in one ear and out the other. Pavielle and Gouch exchanged glances, and then they looked up at their uncle. "We still down!" the boys said in unison.

Present

The Escalade pulled off the road onto the desert ground. It drove about four miles before stopping just outside the shade of a tree. The hatch of the SUV popped open and the doors swung out. Next, Pavielle, Killa Dre and Banga jumped down to the ground. They made their way to the rear of the vehicle, pulling off their shirts and exposing their upper bodies. Pavielle opened the hatch and began passing out shovels. He kept one for himself and grabbed two jugs of water, slamming the hatch closed. He and the fellas were going to have to be hydrated if they hoped to get the task done. It was as hot as an African Laundry mat outside and he was sure that the thirst would creep up on them. He took the time to peer up at the sun. He narrowed his eyes as the bright illumination of the enormous ember shined in his face. Afterwards, he and his homeboys got right to work, digging up a specific spot underneath the shade of the tree.

Two hours later

The sun had dipped below the surface, turning the blue sky a golden hue. The wind blew gently, disturbing the leaves of the tree that the men were digging underneath. All that could be heard were their grunts as they stabbed their shovels into the dirt and scooped up piles of land. Their bodies shined with perspiration as they worked hard plunging their tools into the ground. The sweat rolled off of their arms and chins, dripping from them like a leaking faucet. They were exhausted but they kept at it. It wasn't long before the wind began to dry their forms.

Ping!

Pavielle's head snapped up when his shovel deflected off something hard and metal. A smile stretched across his face as he looked to his homeboys; they were wearing smiles as well. That sound signaled to them that they had hit their buried treasure.

"Y'all niggaz come on, we can get 'em up before the sun dips below ground." Paville said, tightening the gloves on his hands and taking a firm hold of his shovel. "Banga, hit them headlights for me, blood."

After doing as he was told, Banga took a thirsty guzzle from one of the jugs until he'd spent it. He then tossed it aside. He jumped back down inside of the hole that he'd helped dig and scooped up his shovel, joining his niggaz in digging up the prize. The trio didn't stop until they reached the bottom of the barrel. Pavielle tossed his shovel out of the hole upon the surface.

"Yo, let me get that crowbar, homie." Pavielle told Killa Dre, wiping his sweaty forehead with the back of his hand. The young nigga pulled himself out of the ditch, darted to the truck and grabbed a crowbar. He passed it to his homeboy and he didn't waste any time popping the lid on the barrel. It was filled with rubber-band stacks of money. Seeing the content of the barrel brought a smile to Pavielle's face. He quickly placed the lid on the barrel and motioned for his comrades to help him.

"Come on. Help me get this mothafucka up outta here and inside of the truck." Pavielle told his niggaz.

Pavielle and his homies loaded the barrel into the back of the truck. He played the front passenger seat while his niggaz rode in the back with the goods. The entire ride back to the spot all he could think about was his big plans for the money.

Chapter Three

Killa Dre drove through the giant golden gates of Black Jesus' estate and headed up towards his mansion. Stopping outside of the drug lord's door, he killed the engine and Pavielle hopped out. He climbed the steps that lead to the front door of his ex-plug's home flanked by Killa Dre and Banga. Using the brass knocker, he knocked on the front door and waited for someone to answer. A moment later, he heard the chain and locks being undone.

Marisol, Black Jesus' maid, pulled open the door and greeted the trio. She stepped aside and allowed them in over the threshold. After shutting the door, she motioned for them to follow her as she strolled down the corridor, gripping her Uzi with both hands. Once they reached the drug lord's study, she knocked on the door and announced the guests that were there to see him. He told her to come inside; she opened the door and allowed Pavielle and his niggaz into the study.

Pavielle and his niggaz saw Black Jesus behind his desk and Bullet sitting in a chair before it. They looked to have been discussing something before they came in. As soon as Bullet made eye contact with them he rose to his feet, slapping hands with them all. He then stepped aside to allow Pavielle the chair that he was sitting him. Pavielle sat down before his ex-plug and they shook hands.

"How are you doing? I mean, considering the fact." Black Jesus asked. He wanted to know how he was dealing with Gouch's tragic death.

"I'm holding my head." Pavielle admitted. He wasn't trying to show how hurt he was but the look in his eyes betrayed him.

"Good. I got something for you," he reached down beside him and came back up with a shiny gold urn, which he sat on the desk top. He slid it before Pavielle and he pulled it closer to him, cracking a slight grin. This was Gouch's ashes. Pavielle had the drug lord cremate him while he was locked up.

"Thanks, I really appreciate this." He caressed the urn and kissed it. When he pulled back he could see his reflection in it.

"Don't mention it."

There was silence for a time, and then Pavielle spoke again.

"You remember when I hit chu on the jack when I was locked up?"

"Yes. I recall." he nodded.

"You told me that if there were anything that you could do for me not to hesitate to ask."

"This is true."

"I'ma need you to open up the pipeline again."

For a moment there was silence, and then Black Jesus replied. "I would, but you're hot boy right now, Booby. I'm pretty sure that the Feds have you under the microscope."

"Nah, nah, nah, this is not for me." he assured him. "This is for my young nigga, Killa Dre," he threw his hand toward his younger homeboy. "I'm stepping down and he's stepping up."

"You mean you're through?" Black Jesus and Bullet exchanged glances.

"Yep."

"You sure?"

"Positive."

"Well, what're you gonna do?"

"I don't know," he shrugged. "But I do know that I'm taking my family and getting the fuck outta L.A."

"Alright, same deal then?"

"Same deal." he nodded. "When should we make the exchange?"

"Gimmie a couple of days, I'll have my guy get in touch with you."

"Bool," Pavielle and his niggaz headed for the door, but Black Jesus calling him back froze them. "What's up with it?" he threw his head back, watching as the drug lord rolled over to him in a wheelchair. He stopped before him.

"I gottaaaa, shall I say? A welcome home gift for you." he smiled proudly.

"Oh, really?" he switched hands with the urn, putting it up under his right arm.

"Well, where is it?"

"Right this way."

Black Jesus rolled off in his wheelchair with everyone trailing behind him. He rolled up to the basement door and unlocked it through a scanning of a palm print. There was the sound of a large lock clicking undone before the drug lord pushed the door ajar. Next, he pressed a button on the side of the door that converted the staircase into a ramp. Black Jesus went down the ramp with everyone following behind him. Reaching the landing they found someone bond to a chair with a black pillowcase over their head. This was a woman. She was wearing a filthy pink bra and panties. She was shaking so badly that her knees were knocking, piss dripping from between her legs, creating a puddle on the floor. Everyone besides Black Jesus scrunched their noses having smelled the repugnant odor of shit lingering in the air. The basement was dark save for the small window that nearly reached the ceiling. The sunlight that shined in through the glass illuminated the hostage in the chair.

"Fuck is this?" Pavielle's frowning face looked from Black Jesus to the hostage.

The drug lord took the urn from him and sat it on his lap. "Why don't you find out for yourself?"

Pavielle approached the hostage and yanked the pillowcase from over her head. His brows furrowed when he saw the battered and bruised face of Rudy staring up at him. Her tears had mixed in with her blood, making her look like the victim in a horror movie.

Pavielle's head whipped around to Black Jesus confused. "Fuck you got her here for?" his inquiring mind wanted to know.

"You ever wonder how Nightmare knew how to find your grandmother? Well, she told him."

Flashback

Gangsta was disappointed with his nephews' decision. He shook his head as he massaged the bridge of his nose. He had hoped that his little speech would have derailed his nephews from the path in which they were headed, but his monologue had fallen on death's ears. Whether he approved of it or not, they were going to bang. The lifestyle and its influence had them vexed. They wanted into the life no matter what the consequences were.

Gangsta didn't want his nephews' gangbanging because he knew first-hand the hardships that came with it. But at least if they were under his wing he could show them some guidance. The ways of the streets and how to carry themselves; it was fucked up but it was better than letting them run wild in the streets, making up rules as they went.

"Alright then," Gangsta blew hard. "I'm finna go see this dude real quick. I'll be back at 9 o'clock. Ya'll be ready when I get back." He told them, stepping down from the steps and making a beeline for his truck, which was parked in the driveway. Pavielle and Gouch broke out in broad smiles after hearing they would be joining the ranks of the Outlaws that night.

Before long the excitement of tonight's initiation had worn off and the boys found themselves lounging in their bedroom, swamped in their thoughts. Their chests were tight with anxiety and their bellies fluttered with butterflies; they *were on the edge about what the night would bring. They had seen niggaz quoted on the set before and they knew there was one of two things that would solidify your membership: you could either be jumped in for 20 seconds or put in some work, if not both. It was all up to the sets ranking members, O.G niggaz like Bully, Monk, Birdman and Gangsta. But whatever the tests were the brothers vowed to pass them with flying colors.*

"What time is it, Gouch?" Pavielle asked.

"8:58," Gouch glanced at the clock on the dresser.

"Damn, man, I can't wait to get this shit over with!" Pavielle vented his frustration.

The anticipation of their forthcoming initiation was killing him and Gouch, but Gouch wasn't letting it show. Being that he was the oldest, and Pavielle looked up to him, almost as much as he did Gangsta, he had to save face.

Hearing someone honking their horn like a madman, Pavielle and Gouch snapped to attention. They picked themselves up and bolted from out of their bedroom and out into the corridor. They ran down the steps of the house and to the truck waiting for them at the curb. Gouch opened the back door of his uncle's SUV and he and Pavielle stashed themselves in the backseat. The Truck took off down Adams as if its passengers had just pulled a bank heist.

***

Gangsta's truck pulled into a dark alley infested with broken glass and discarded trash. Pavielle strained his eyes trying to peer through the tinted windows and see exactly where they were. Upon further inspection, he realized they were in an alley. He knew the 20s like the back of his hand but the alley was alien to him. Unbeknownst to him, he had been there before but that was when the sun was out. No one had dared to step foot in the alley on 21st and Griffith.

A few years ago a couple of kids on their way home from school had found a rotten, severed head in a mop bucket there. The head was swarming with flies, and maggots had made a home in its eye sockets. You could still see the mold of a man attempting to scream on its face. Just a few feet away inside of a dumpster was the decapitated body that the head was once attached to. The hands and feet of the body had been hacked off as well. The mutilated body smelled something awful. It smelled like a sack full of assholes.

There was a rumor going around in The Bottoms that the dismembered body belonged to a man named Hector Sezma. The Latino had run afoul the Mexican mafia. He was hustling heroin on turf already spoken for. When he was given his warning to stop, he didn't comply so the Chicanos sicced The Ghost on him. If there were three things you didn't want to catch in life, it was: AIDS, a RICO case, and wind that one of the deadliest assassins in the America was after you.

"Where are we?" Pavielle asked from the backseat.

"Y'all hop out!" Gangsta unlocked the truck's doors. The boys hopped out of the truck and approached the tall sliding gate. The gate was covered with all kinds of crap you might find in a junkyard. The openings of the gate were covered so well that you couldn't steal a peek of the house that sat beyond it. And that's just how its owner wanted it.

Gangsta honked his horn twice before rolling off down the alley. Pavielle and Gouch waited a while to see if someone would appear to open the gate and let them in. About a minute had passed before they tried to pull the gate open themselves. It was heavy from all the junk attached to it. So it took a while for the boys to slide it open wide enough for them to wiggle through. After pulling the gate closed, the brothers turned around and it registered to them where they were: O.G Bully's backyard. There wasn't a soul in sight. It was dark and quiet too; all Pavielle and Gouch could hear were their the crickets in the unkempt lawn.

Bully's backyard was spooky, Pavielle couldn't shake the feeling that some maniac was going to spring out of nowhere with a machete and come after them. The young man's vivid imagination was quickly put at ease once the garage door opened. A tall, muscular man slithered out taking pulls from a blunt as he advanced in their direction. It was dark out so the boys couldn't see exactly who it was approaching them. The closer the man drew, the more his facial features filled out. Gouch and Pavielle gave the man standing before them the once over. The boys knew him by face and reputation, a reputation they hoped to garner for themselves.

"Soowoo," Bully greeted Pavielle and Gouch behind lazy bloodshot eyes. He held a burning blunt in one hand and used the other to slap hands with the boys. Bully was a dark skinned brother with a muscular build who wore his hair in box-braids. He'd been a jack boy until Gangsta put him onto the drug game as his enforcer and made him retire his ski-mask.

"Soowoo, blood," Pavielle and Gouch replied in unison. They were familiar with the O.G standing before them. He was Gangsta's best friend and somewhat of an uncle to them. To them, he was right alongside Gangsta; a figure in their lives who was bigger than life.

Pavielle and Gouch a pair of hands grip their shoulders. They looked over their shoulders and Gangsta was standing over them. They didn't even hear him slide open the gate and ooze inside. For a big dude he was quite stealthy and limber. As swift as he was the boys knew if they were his enemies they'd already be dead.

"Now, y'all uncle tells me y'all want in on this thing of ours," Bully continued, passing the blunt to Gangsta who'd just came to stand beside him. The boys nodded yes. "I've been hearing whispers around the hood about y'all. The homies saying y'all some down lil' Gs, on duce owe. We'd be happy to have y'all pushing the turf. But, as y'all know, there aren't any walk-ons, so you're gonna have to put in some work. So, what's up? Y'all lil' niggaz down for a one-eighty seven?" he looked back and forth between the young men.

"Nigga what?" Pavielle began. "What, you ain't know? Twenty-six street niggaz been about that action."

"All day," Gouch nodded. "I've been waiting to put the flames to a nigga." He made his hand into the shape of a gun, gripped it with the other, and said, Pow! This caused Bully to laugh.

"Y'all follow me." Bully waved them on as he headed into the garage. Once inside he gave the boys two black hoodies and told them to put them on. He stepped into a black jumpsuit and grabbed a rusty red toolbox from the corner of the garage. He popped the locks on it and removed the tray of screws and bolts, revealing an arsenal of handguns. The serial numbers were filed off of the weapons. Though they were scarred and bruised they worked like new.

"Y'all dig in, grab whatever you want." Bully told Pavielle and Gouch.

When Pavielle and Gouch saw all of the guns in the toolbox they knew shit had gotten serious. They were about to leave the little leagues and sign up to play with the big boys. It was time to put that work in and earn their stripes and their rites of passage into hood stardom. The boys dug into the toolbox as if they were looking for the prize at the bottom of a cereal box. Gouch picked up a .45 automatic and Pavielle grabbed a Glock.

Gangsta returned to the garage from taking a piss. His murder gear was a black Dickie suit and black wool gloves, which were stuffed in his shirt pocket. Bully removed two Uzi .9mms from under the mattress of the twin bed: one was black and the other was chrome. He kept the chrome one for himself and gave the black one to Gangsta. Gangsta checked the *magazine for a fully loaded clip before cocking the hammer on it.*

Pavielle looked at his uncle and saw his bloodshot and glassy eyes. At first, he thought they were that way from the effects of the weed but something inside of him told him otherwise. He realized that his uncle had been crying, which he hadn't seen him do since his father's passing. Pavielle knew why his uncle had been grieving. And the only way he could stop it is if he and Gouch didn't go through with the night's initiation. As much as the boys loved their uncle it was no way in hell they were pulling out of the mission now. They'd gotten too close to their dreams to not see them come true.

Glock held at his side, Pavielle approached his uncle. "You alright?"

"Yeah, I'm good, and you?" Gangsta asked.

Pavielle shrugged. "I'm straight."

Gangsta managed a smile and ruffled Pavielle's head. "You straight, huh? Gucci," he called his eldest nephew. "Come over here, I wanna say a quick prayer before we get outta here." Gouch joined the twosome and they bowed their heads.

Gangsta was just about to start the prayer when Pavielle spoke.

"Yo, O.G, you're not joining us for prayer?"

"Nah, lil' homie, I put all my faith in this here." *Bully cocked the hammer on his Uzi .9mm and kissed it.*

"Y'all close your eyes and bow your heads." *Gangsta told his nephews as he placed his hands on their shoulders. He cleared his throat and began his prayer.* "Heavenly Father, we gather here tonight to ask that chu watch over us as we prepare to enter battle. Cloak us in your blood, Lord; shield us from enemy fire. I know that what we're about to do is wrong and one day we will answer for our actions. But I ask that on this night, you guide us through this terrible sin we go forth to commit. I ask that you allow me, my homeboy, and my nephews to return home in one peace. Our father who art in heaven, Amen," *He turned to Bully.* "You ready?"

"I stay ready, blood. Let's roll."

Present

After Black Jesus told him that Rudy was the one that had given Nightmare his grandmother's address, Pavielle whipped his head around to her. She was scared like hell and more piss was raining from between her legs.

"Is that right?" the young kingpin's eyebrows lowered and he tightened his jaws so much they pulsated. He watched as she continued to cry and shake her head, no. "Yes, you did. Stop lying you treacherous bitch!" he smacked Rudy across the face so hard that her head whipped around, sending her unkempt braids flying up into the air.

Pavielle's palm stung from the smack that he delivered across the crackhead's face. He stood over the hostage, nostrils flaring and chest jumping. His head darted all over the basement looking for something that he could use to finish the job. He smiled devilishly when he saw several golf clubs sticking out from a bag in the corner. Speed walking over to the bag, he snatched the golf club out that had the bigger head. He marveled its craftsmanship, test swinging it for a second before storming back over to Rudy who was still in a daze. Standing to the side with the golf club outstretched to the floor, he cocked back and swung that bitch at Rudy's head. The gold club swooshed through the air, en route toward its mark.

Cling!

The vicious blow snapped Rudy's head to the side and sent her braids flying again. Blood ran from the side of her head and stained her breasts. He swung the club again and knocked her bottom jaw out of place, it moved awkwardly. He launched the club again and split open the center of her forehead, causing blood to drench her face. Her eyes rolled all around inside of her head as it bobbled about. Breathing harder than he was before, Pavielle stood before his victim and lifted the club above his head. With all of his might, he swung it down at the top of her skull. The impact sounded like a walnut being cracked. Seeing that she was dead, he wiped his fingerprints clean of the golf club and tossed it aside.

"Welcome home, Booby." Black Jesus smiled, clapping his hands, like he'd just watched an incredible performance on stage and the curtains were just closed.

"It feels good to be back." Pavielle thanked the drug lord and picked up the urn from off of his lap. He caressed the side of the golden vase and then kissed it lovingly. Afterwards, he motioned for his niggaz to follow him and they followed suit.

There's no place like home.

Chapter Four

The sun had set and allowed darkness to lay its claim to the streets. Banga had just coasted over the railroad tracks from Watts heading over into Compton. The first thing Pavielle took notice of was the smell of weed in the air, gunshots sounding off in the distance, and barking dogs. Niggaz was kicking it and indulging in their poison of choice, while the occasional car that passed through played loud music from the latest hip hop phenomenon.

Pavielle, Banga and Killa Dre took in their surroundings, feeling quite comfortable. The Hub City's environment wasn't anything new to them. Hell, it actually mimicked their own. It was like their home away from home having been there so many times to a gangsta party or politic with other sets. No one was more familiar than Banga was with this part of Los Angeles County though. This was because he had spent half of his life here with his grandparents. They were the ones that had raised him and Playboy from pups to dogs.

Banga traveled down Central Avenue and made a right on 120th street. Coming to the middle of the residential block, he made a left into the driveway of a copper brown house that had black iron bars on all of the windows. A rusty fence surrounded the dirt patched lawn. As Banga was turning off the Escalade, Pavielle took a look out of the window, staring up at the roof of the house. It was there that he saw two young niggaz in hoods wearing bandanas over the lower halves of their faces. He spotted them sitting down and holding AK-47s, watching the block. It wasn't until they saw the truck pulling up that they hurried to their feet.

"Yo, who these niggaz on the roof, man," Pavielle frowned, pointing to the roof of the house as he questioned Banga. He tucked his urn under his arm and continued to stare up at the niggaz on the rooftop with the choppas.

"You mean them young ass niggaz on the rooftop there? That's security." Banga answered him. "I put 'em there to keep wifey and junior safe. I gotta couple mo' of my people on the porch too, they don't play. You know how these Compton niggaz get down."

"Two sho'." he nodded in agreement.

"Y'all come on." Banga opened up the door and hopped out of the car.

Pavielle and Killa Dre jumped out of the whip behind him. They mobbed inside of the yard of the house behind Banga. Nearing the front porch, they saw two more niggaz sitting in chair with Uzis in their laps. They wore hard faces. One rocked a beanie with Compton emblazoned on the front of it, while the other sported a snapback with the same city emblazoned on it.

Banga stepped upon the porch and slapped hands with the niggaz out front holding it down with them thangz.

"Killa, Booby," he looked back at his homeboys and then to the two dudes on the porch. "These are my relatives, Tay and Mad Man." he introduced everyone. Everyone gave each other nods of respect and exchanged daps. Afterwards, Banga explained to his people who Booby was and who Vayda and baby Nasheed were to him. From there, Booby tried breaking bread with them, but they wouldn't take anything from him.

"Nah, nah, nah," Tay waved him off, "Yo' money ain't no good here."

"Fa real though, this is all love out here," Mad Man told him.

"I appreciate that, fam. Straight up, that's some real shit." he pounded his fist against his chest.

"You know what chu could probably do for us, though, my nigga?"

"Speak on it, dawg."

"My people says you're handling, I was thinking that you can cut me and my relative a nice price on a couple of them thangz."

Pavielle looked back and forth between Banga and his people. He nodded and said, "Alright, bool. Once I get right, I'ma get chu right." he took the cellular that Tay gave him and programmed his name and number into it. Right after, he passed it back to him.

Banga passed Pavielle the key to the house. He and Killa Dre decided to kick it outside with his relatives to give the young kingpin some time alone with his family.

Pavielle stepped inside of the house and pulled the door shut behind him, stashing the key inside the pocket of his jeans. Standing where he was, he took in the scenery of the house. It was scarcely furnished. There was black leather furniture and a big screen TV. A PlayStation 4 sat on the floor below the television set. The house was quiet save for the occasional beeping of the dysfunctional smoke detector and the TV going behind the bedroom door. Looking to the bedroom's door, Pavielle could see the blue illumination of the television's screen in the opening at the bottom of the door.

Pavielle's bowed lips formed a smile that stretched across his face. He knew behind that door resided his family. Stepping to the door, he lifted his fist and knocked on it, holding the urn under his arm. Placing his ear toward the door, he listened for a time to see if anyone was going to come open the door. When no one came to answer, he turned the knob and entered the room. Standing in the doorway, he watched as Vayda lie in bed with their baby boy beside her fast asleep. He couldn't believe his eyes. When he entered through those gates of hell, he thought he'd never see them again unless it was behind Plexiglas. But nah, that wasn't the case. Here they were. Right here in front of him, looking more beautiful than they had ever before to him.

Pavielle sat the urn down in the corner of the bedroom and cupped the lower half of his face. His eyes misted with tears and they came rolling down his cheeks as soon as he blinked his eyelids. His shoulders shuddered and he broke down sobbing. He placed his hand on the television set and turned away from his family, crying his eyes out. He looked up at the ceiling with glassy, pink eyes and mouthed 'Thank you, Lord. Thank you for letting me come home to my family.' Right after he did this, he broke down again, sobbing louder than he did previously. It was like a miracle to be back home again. He owed all of the praise in the world to Gouch, because if it wasn't for his sacrifice he knew that he wouldn't be there right then.

"Pavy?" Vayda awoke from her sleep groggily and narrowing her eyelids. She leaned her head closer trying to make out who it was standing by the TV. The blue flashes coming from the television shined on and off his face as a commercial played on the screen. When he looked to her and she recognized that it really was him, she hopped out of bed and ran into his arms. They both broke down crying and kissing, confessing their love for one another over and over again. She found herself touching his face like he wasn't real as tears ran down her cheeks in a hurry. "It's...It's really you, baby. I can't believe it, you're really here, but how?" the tips of her delicate fingers caressed his face. He took her hand and kissed the inside of her palm tenderly. He then gripped the back of her neck and pulled her closer, kissing her romantically.

"I'll explain everything later." he told her. "Right now, I wanna take a hot bath to cleanse this jailhouse funk off of me."

"Okay. I'll draw you a bath." she cupped his face and kissed him twice more on his lips. After giving him one last hug, she headed off to the bathroom to do what she'd told him she was.

Once Vayda was out of sight, Pavielle approached the bed smiling having seen his son sleeping. He sat down on the bed beside him and caressed his crown of dark curly hair lovingly. He thought he'd never love anyone as much as he loved Vayda, but he couldn't have been so wrong. The joy he experienced from holding his first born was second to none. Absolutely nothing could beat out that moment in time. Not even when the day comes when he marries Vayda.

Pavielle sat perched where he was, stroking his son's hair and singing him a lullaby.

"Baby," Vayda called for him from the bathroom's doorway. He looked to find her with a towel so small that it left little to the imagination. She looked so sexy standing there with her curly hair covering half of her face and smiling seductively. "Your bath is ready."

"Okay, I'll be right there." He told her, watching as she sauntered off. After kissing his son on the head, Pavielle made his way inside of the bathroom. He pulled his strap off his waistline with one hand and used the other to unbuckle his black leather belt. Turning slightly to the right, he kicked the door shut.

***

A glistening Vayda lay back in the tub with Pavielle's head lying against her bosom. They were both submerged in the sudsy water which was so hot that it was giving off vapors. The couple's eyelids were closed and they had smirks on their faces, enjoying the temperature of the water.

"So what's next, kingpin?" Vayda brought her head up from the tub. She wrapped her arms around him and kissed him on the side of the face.

"I'm out, shit. That's what's next," he assured her, sounding confident.

Vayda gave him a disbelieving expression. "Come on now, let's be serious."

"I am. I'm done with this shit." he tried to convince her. "Them crackas cleaned my black ass out and left me flat broke. Not to mention they scared the shit outta me with all of that time they were tryna hit me with."

"Damn," she looked away thinking and shaking her head pitifully.

"What's up?" he looked to her, holding onto her arms.

"I can't believe they got cho brotha."

He turned back around, not wanting her to see him cry if need be. "Me either. Shit don't seem real, but Gucci is gone."

"Yeah, I'm sorry, baby. I'm really, really sorry."

"It's okay."

"What're we gonna do?"

"I got some money that I put up. We gone take that and get out of here on the first thang smoking."

"You serious?" she cracked a grin. The streets were crazy as hell and she wanted her family out of them ASAP, before they all became a statistic.

"Yes." he nodded.

"When can we leave?"

"Whenever you wanna leave."

"Okay." she smiled as she thought on it, "How about tomorrow morning? We can still catch that flight to Miami. I've never been there, and I'd love to go."

Pavielle's face transformed into one of disappointment because he didn't want to tell her anything that would hurt her.

The smile disappeared from off Vayda's face seeing the expression her man was wearing. "Lemmie guess, you can't leave then right?" she frowned up and pushed him up off of her, climbing out of the tub dripping wet.

"Nah, I can't."

"And why is that?" she wiped the tears from out of her eyes with one hand and swiped the towel down from off the rack, drying herself off.

"I gotta get these fools back that killed my brotha." he stood up in the tub naked and dripping water, causing small waves of water to ripple on the surface.

Vayda's face balled up and she blew hot air. She looked up at the ceiling pissed off, wiping away her tears. "Why can't we just go, huh? Why can't we just grab the baby, pack up our shit and go? If we stay here then I'm gonna eventually be burying you and I don't want that to happen."

"Baby, you gotta believe me when I tell you that's not gone happen." his face took on a more serious look. "I'm telling you, as soon as I smash these niggaz that crushed my brotha, we're outta here. We're getting the fuck outta L.A and we ain't never looking back."

"You just don't get it do you?" she looked at him with tears pouring down her face in buckets. "How many times have you escaped prison and death, huh? Sooner or later, something is gonna stick. And you're gonna leave me and your son, your prince," she pointed at the door that baby

Nasheed was behind. "Alone. Alone is this cold world that doesn't have any mercy for anybody."

"Goddamn it!" he punched a hole in the wall, startling her. "What is it that you want me to do, huh? Turn my back on everything and dip off into the sunset witchu? Let my brotha's killers walk away? Leave my niggaz out here without a way to eat? Leave the niggaz that's been riding and dying with me for so long out here to starve? Nah, fuck that! It ain't happening like that! I'ma honorable man," he slapped his hand up against his wet chest. "And I can't leave my soldiers out here to…"his words died in his throat seeing her drop down to her hands and knees, crying her eyes out. She looked to be in great pain, great emotional pain. The thought of losing him had her scared out of her mind. She could just see her future husband lying face up in a coffin and herself holding their baby, sobbing. Damn, it all felt so real to her, like she was right there in the flesh. She could hear the organs cry as the pianist played funeral music, as well as the weeping of Pavielle's friends and family.

Pavielle kneeled down to her and cupped her face, looking into her eyes. "Look at me, babe. Once I whack these niggaz that got at my brotha, and close this deal with this plug for Killa, we gone, we outta here, bae. We getting the fuck outta Killa Cali and we're not eva looking back, you hear me?" She nodded her head and tears came bursting out of her eyes, sliding down her cheeks. As bad as she wanted to she couldn't stop them from coming. Out of the blue, she hugged him tight. They stood there in the bathroom in the nude, wrapped in one another's arms. Her body trembled in his strong embrace as she shed her grievance and he caressed her back. "It's gone be alright, ma. I just need you to hold it down for me, okay? Alright?" he said, holding her away from him and looking into her eyes.

"Alright." she nodded, sniffling. "I'ma hold it down. I am your rider." he smiled proudly, believing that as long as he had his family by his side that he could get through anything that was thrown at him in life, absolutely anything. "I only ask that you do one thing for me."

"Anything," he stared deep into her bluish green eyes, caressing her chin with his thumb. "Anything you want from me. All you gotta do is name it and it's yours."

"Marry me."

He frowned. "Marry you? Baby, that's already happening."

"No. Marry me tomorrow."

"Tomorrow?"

"Yes. You said anything and that's what I want."

"Okay. That's what it is then. Tomorrow you'll official be Mrs. Hood."

After drying off and getting dressed, the couple climbed into bed with their sleeping baby. They snuggled up together and shut their eyes. Pavielle peeled his eyelids back open and kissed his family on their foreheads before getting comfortable. It wasn't long before the Sandman came for them all.

The next morning, Vayda made a big breakfast that fed everyone in the house. Killa Dre, Banga, Tay, Mad Man, all of them niggaz ate real good. Because homegirl could get busy in the kitchen with those pots and pans. Afterwards, Pavielle shot to the Del Amo mall where he got a couple of gold wedding bands with 'I am yours' and 'you are mine' engraved on the insides of them. While he was out doing this, Banga was procuring the minister from the church at the end of the block from where Pavielle's family where holed up. Minister Jeffrey Cash had been residing over the church since Banga and Playboy were little and their grandparents were attending.

The hood was sure that the minister would marry the kingpin and his wifey for a nice donation to the church. About two hours later, the living room was full with everyone that had been there the night before. Pavielle and Vayda stood there before the minister, hand and hand. They smiled as they listened to him spit his truths. His last words were...

"I now pronounce you husband and wife. You may kiss the bride." Minister Cash smiled, looking from Pavielle to Vayda as they kissed lovingly. He patted his sweaty forehead with a neatly folded handkerchief. Everyone in the living room applauded and looked on.

Banga slipped the minister a hefty envelope in which he slipped inside of the recess of his robe. They chopped it up as he walked him to his Cadillac and sent him off, waving as the black on black vehicle drove off. Afterwards, he headed back inside of the house where they were eating the wedding cake. Once everyone had cake, they ate at a Chinese takeout joint not far from the house. With Pavielle and Vayda officially being married, it was time to get down to business. The squad got vested up and strapped down so they could move out to the meeting. It was very important that this meeting take place because it was essential to Pavielle exacting his revenge.

Chapter Five

Vayda stood looking out of the window as Pavielle and his niggaz backed out of the driveway. She was cradling her beautiful baby boy in her arm when she locked eyes with her lover, blowing him a sweet kiss. He smirked as he caught it and smacked it over his heart. He mouthed 'I love you' and she mouthed it back. Having drawn the curtains closed, she walked across the living room admiring her son as he stared up at her with those marvelous eyes of his, smiling and flailing his limbs. She smiled at him and tapped the tip of his nose. Sitting down on the couch, she threw a towel over her shoulder and popped her breast out. She brought her baby to her nipple and he immediately began sucking on it. She caressed his curly head as he fed; humming a soothing tune that only mother's could to their child.

Vayda couldn't believe where she was in life now. She thought she would have been dead by now, but the good Lord didn't see it in his cards for her just yet. She gathered that he must have been looking out for her since he knew all of the hell that she'd been through. She had been physically and mentally broken by her ex-pimp, Buddy. The things that he did to her and allowed to happen to her, lead her to believe that he was the devil reincarnated.

Vayda thought back to a horrifying time in her life that she'd remember until the day she died. Any other woman would have broken, but she wasn't your average woman. Nah, she was a survivor. Shit, that's what she'd been doing all of her life…surviving.

Flashback

Buddy pulled into the driveway of his home and Crystal, one of his whores, came running out. Her hair was a mess and her right-eye was blackened. Her face was shiny from sweat. From the looks of her you could tell that she had been fighting.

"Bitch, what the fuck is wrong with you?" Buddy asked. He addressed her as 'bitch' like it was her government.

"Daddy, this ho in there tripping, talking about she's leaving." Crystal breathed heavily, looking at him through the driver side window.

"Who?"

"Vayda," Crystal informed him. "Talking about she tired of this lifestyle and putting up with you. I told her she's not going no mothafucking where without your say so. And she said 'oh, yeah?' And I said, 'bitch I'm not in the habit of repeated myself' and she punched me dead in my mothafucking eye. You know it was on then. We started scrapping like cats and dogs. Then the bitch bit me on my left-titty, ran into her room and slammed the door shut behind her."

"So, redbone think she's just gone step out on a nigga, huh?" Buddy's eyebrows arched and his nose scrunched up.

"Yeah, she's up there packing right now." Crystal folded her arms across her chest and tapped her flip flopped feet impatiently, waiting to see what her pimp was going to do.

"This bitch done lost her mind. Move out my way, bitch!" Buddy swung open the door and headed towards the house. He was hot as a mothafucka, making plans to beat Vayda's ass as soon as he laid eyes on her.

***

Vayda picked both of her suitcases up from the floor and headed for the door.

Boom!

The door was kicked open with a force so brutal that it sent a spray of wood shards and debris everywhere. Vayda was startled, not to mention surprised when she saw her pimp standing in the doorway. She hadn't expected to see him back so soon.

Seeing murder in Buddy's eyes, Vayda slowly began to step back. She looked around the room for an escape route and her eyes settled on the window. She dropped her suitcases and ran over to the window. She tried to pull it open but it wouldn't budge.

"Bitch, where the fuck you think you're going?" Buddy grabbed a lock on Vayda's hair and she swung on him. The blow connected but Buddy took it like a champ. He got into a boxing stance and threw up fists. Vayda held up her hands, sobbing and pleading. Buddy wasn't trying to hear that shit, though. A devilish smile broadened his face. He loved handing down discipline to his whores when they got out of pocket.

"Uh huh, you wanna fight a nigga and shit, huh, bitch? Put cho mothafucking hands up!"

"Daddy, I'm sorry. I didn't mean to do it." Vayda cried, hands trembling. She was in fear of what he would do for her swinging on him.

"Swing, bitch, gone and swing again, 'cause I'ma knock your ass out anyway."

Crystal watched from the doorway as Vayda swung on Buddy again. This time, he ducked her swing and threw a mean ass three punch combination to her head. The accurate punches left the redbone bleeding from the mouth. Buddy *moved in for the finish. He gave her two body shots and a right hook that sent her crashing to the floor, unconscious.*

***

While in a coma Vayda could hear the furniture being moved about in the bedroom. She heard the bed, the nightstands and the dresser as they were slid across the old hardwood floor. She could hear Buddy, too. He was helping Crystal move everything around. She listened as they struggled to bring something large and heavy up the stairs. She heard a lot of racket, mainly noisy tools as they were put to use.

About an hour later she was stripped naked. She felt a cool breeze that ruffled the stubble on her pussy. She felt the hot vapors of water and the smell of Dove soap. She flinched as a damp washcloth touched her body. At first she was tense, but she relaxed once the cloth began its tour of her body, cleaning every inch of her. Its warmth felt good on her skin. The cloth was dunked into a bucket of soap and water and then wrung out. She gave a soft moan as it dabbed her wounded face, picking up the dry blood as it went along. Once the bath was done, the bather dropped the cloth into the bucket and handcuffed Vayda to the post of her bed. Vayda listened as the bather left the room, carrying the bucket along with them.

Sometime later, Vayda began to come to. She heard two people talking. She knew one of the voices was Buddy's but she didn't know who the other belonged to. She blinked her eyes twice and looked around, discovering that her vision was distorted. All she could make out was smeared colors. One of the colors was golden brown and the other was pink. She figured the golden brown one was Buddy and the pink was some white man.

The white man paid Buddy and he left. The white man sat his brim on the nightstand and he straddled Vayda. Once he forced her legs open she knew what he planned to do but she was too weak to stop him. She felt the white man enter her dry vagina, and thanked God he was wearing a condom. She closed her eyes tight, feeling him pump and sweat on top of her. Three minutes later, he exploded into the condom and feeling it with his warm semen, collapsing on top of her. Vayda could feel his hot, damp flesh and his pounding heartbeat against her own.

Shortly thereafter, the white man got dressed and left. Vayda opened her eyes and her vision had returned. She looked around her bedroom; it had been converted into a *prison. The windows had been boarded up and there was a thick metal-door in place of the wood one. The floor was bare; the only furniture on it was her queen size bed, which she was handcuffed to.*

For the next couple of months, Vayda was made to have sex with fifty-two men against her will. At first, she fought it but her struggles were futile. So, she let her mind take her to a happier place and time. She watched her movie play behind her eyelids. When the movie would get to the part where everything went wrong in her life, she'd rewind it to the beginning. It was the only thing that kept her from going insane.

Vayda would eat very little when she was fed, not because she was being rebellious. But because she was trying to lose enough weight so she could slip out of the handcuffs. Days went by and Vayda had lost a considerable amount of weight. So much that she could almost slide her wrist from the metal bracelet. She figured a few more days of rations and her wrist would be slender enough to escape the handcuffs. She knew that once she was free that she'd definitely need a weapon to defend herself with. So she worked a piece of metal loose from the bedspring and fashioned it to a point on the edge of the iron-frame bed. Once the metal was sharpened to her liking, she practiced jabbing it into the mattress. The shank penetrated the mattress with ease. Satisfied with the weapon she had crafted, she made a hole on the side of the mattress and stashed it there. She then closed her eyes for a goodnight's rest.

***

The sun's rays shined in on Vayda's face through the openings of the boarded up windows welcoming her to the next morning. Her eyes fluttered open and she looked around. Her eyes settled on the boarded up windows. The sun was shining its brightest so she knew it had to be afternoon. Hearing the locks of the metal door being undone, Vayda pretended to be asleep.

The metal door swung open and Buddy and a fat trucker walked in. The fat trucker was about 5 '7 with a round, pie face and sunburned skin. He licked his chops and rubbed his meaty hands together once he saw Vayda lying on the bed. He was pleased with the eye candy that lay before him.

"She sure is purrty," The fat trucker said. "How much?"

"Two hundred, boss," Buddy held out his hand and wiggled his fingers. The fat trucker smacked two crinkled one hundred dollar bills into his palm. Buddy straightened them out as best as he could and held them up towards the light to check their authenticity. Satisfied with the bills, he shoved them into his pocket and left the fat trucker with Vayda.

The fat trucker removed his cap and stripped down to his wife-beater and boxers. Vayda stared into the unknown as he straddled her, sloppily sucking on her neck and breasts. As he licked and sucked the nipple of her right-breast, his fingers crept their way down her torso and stopped at her pussy. He slipped his stubby fingers in and out of her trying to work her to moisture, but she didn't give.

"Boy, you're as dry as the Sahara Desert down there, darling." He harped up some phlegm and spat it in his palm, using it to lather up his manhood. Afterwards, he pushed himself between her walls of heaven. The fat trucker grunted and his eyes rolled. Vayda's hole felt so good to him that he couldn't wait to fill it with his semen. He went in and out of her vagina, grunting as he pumped away feverishly. While he was handling his business Vayda slipped her homemade shank from its hiding place. She decided to let the fat trucker have his last organism as a parting gift before he met his maker. The fat trucker went as fast as he could, sliding in and out of her. He was working toward his nut with a psycho's fury.

"*Oh, momma, here I come!*" the trucker made noises like a wounded whale and then unleashed his spunk deep inside of her womb. An expression of sensual pleasure and satisfaction ceased his face once he relieved himself. Right thereafter, with a grunt, Vayda drove the long, crooked 7 inch shank into the fat trucker's neck. His face turned beet red and the sensual pleasure on his face gave way to a mask of excruciating agony. The trucker's eyes stretched wide open and his mouth formed an O, his life's blood spraying out of the side of his neck. The blood drenched Vayda's upper half and she squeezed her eyes shut and gritted her teeth.

 Vayda's eyes burned with a mortal hatred for the man on top of her as she twisted and dug her shank in his neck. The mothafucka gagged and gargled on the blood that pooled inside of his mouth. His eyes then rolled to their corners and his tongue hung out of his mouth grotesquely. At that moment, Vayda clenched her jaws tight and broke her homemade shank off in his neck. She then kicked him off of her and he landed on the floor. He lay there still on his belly, blood pooling beneath his lifeless form.

 Vayda tried to work her wrist out of the handcuff but she couldn't free herself. So she spat as much saliva as she could on her wrist and lubed it up. Finally, she was able to free herself from the confines of the metal bracelet.

There was a rap on the metal door.

"What the fuck is going on in there? Open this goddamn door!" Buddy yelled from the other side of the door. Vayda raced over to the boarded up window and began prying the 2x4s off. Vayda was on the last 2x4 when she heard the rattling of keys at the door. She knew she had to hurry now.

After freeing the last 2x4 from over the window, Vayda tried to lift the window but it wouldn't budge. So she ran to the back of the bedroom, got into a runner's position and ran towards the window, just as the metal door was coming open. Vayda leapt towards the window and the glass exploded as she went through it. She crashed onto the front lawn with glass and wood shards raining down upon her. The bottom of Vayda's foot was on fire. She looked and there was a gash so deep on the bottom of her foot that she could see the bone. Hopping up on one foot, she looked up at the window she leapt through and met the scowl of her pimp.

Buddy withdrew his gun and Vayda ran as fast as one foot could carry her. The pimp drew a bead on her and pulled the trigger. A bullet ripped through her shoulder and she collapsed to the ground, bleeding.

Present

Yes, sir, that was a memory that would be with Vayda forever. The bullet was still lodged in her from that very day. When she went to the hospital and a couple of detectives came around asking questions, she told them she was leaving the house to go out on a date with her boyfriend, Buddy, and fucked around and caught a stray from a drive by. The detectives didn't believe it but they weren't about to press her any further. They decided to drop it and go about their business.

That very same night Buddy, Crystal and her drained the trucker's body in the bath tub and chopped him up, placing his severed body parts into black garbage bags. They took the bags out into the woods somewhere and buried them deep where no one would ever find them. After that incident Vayda was fearful of Buddy and what he'd do to her should she ever tried to leave him again. It wasn't until the last incident had taken place that she decided to revolt. This situation led her back out west to South Central Los Angeles, or what the locals refer to as South Central Los Scandalous.

That night

An Escalade pulled up underneath the freeway and its driver executed its engine. Hopping out from front passenger seat, Pavielle heard the sound of vehicles whipping back and forth overhead. The weather that night was crisp and cool. This is why he'd donned a beanie and a dookie brown Dickie suit, which he wore underneath a hefty jacket. Pavielle slammed the door shut and stashed his hands inside of his pockets, going to stand in front of the grill of the truck.

"Yo, you want us to post up out there witchu?" Banga asked from behind the wheel as he took casual pulls from his thinly rolled blunt. He was referring to himself and that nigga Killa Dre who was chilling in the backseat, nodding his head to the music and keeping a firm grip on his Death Dealer. If some shit popped off, he was going to stop a nigga from breathing.

"Nah, ya'll good, Blood, this ain't nothing for y'all to sweat." Pavielle said over his shoulder. Banga went back to smoking his weed and turned up the volume on the stereo, nodding his head to The Dogg Pound's *Let's play house.*

Just then, bright headlights invaded the area, shining in on Pavielle and the Escalade. An old box Chevy Trailblazer pulled up before him and its engine died. Pavielle could feel the warmth of the truck emitting from underneath its hood. This let him know that the nigga that he was meeting with had driven a long distance. He had that nigga Lester do his homework on homeboy and he found out that he was living out in

Riverside. Through his investigation he discovered that the man had a wife, four kids, a cat and a dog. Not to mention that his ill grandmother was staying with him. This cat was definitely a good flag saluting mothafucka that was living the life the American way. Pavielle found this to be odd seeing as how homeboy was an ex-knucklehead.

Fuller hopped out of his SUV dressed to combat the weather in a Pirates fitted cap that he wore cocked to the side and a hoodie. An icy gold Jesus piece dangled from his neck and pounced off his chest with each step that he took in his Air Jordan's 13. He threw his head back slightly and gnawed on his toothpick, slapping hands with Pavielle. The young kingpin drunk him in and realized that the way he was dressed made him look nothing like the nigga he knew back at the county jail, patrolling the facility.

"Humph." Pavielle cracked a smirk and dimpled his cheek.

You can take a nigga out of the hood but you can't take the hood out of a nigga, he thought.

"What's up with it, Boss Dawg." Fuller greeted him.

"Ain't shit," he shook his head. "You got that work for me, homie?" he questioned. Fuck the small talk. He was ready to get down to business.

"Yeah, I got chu, G. Step into my office," he motioned for him to follow him with a manila envelope, stepping before the grill of his truck. Once his employer was standing beside him, Fuller pulled out six mug shots, all of which were of the inmates that had murdered Gouch and threw his ass over the guardrail.

Fuller placed six photographs flat on the hood of his Chevy. He set the manila envelope aside and went on to tell who each man in the photos was.

"This is Miguel 'Capo' Hernandez, Hector 'Poe Boy' Guzman, Fernando 'Chop' Ruiz, Juan 'Monsta' Rodriguez, Victor 'Midget' Perez, and Jonathan 'Nino' Salazar."

Pavielle took the time to study each and every face on the photos presented before him. Right there on the spot, the day of Gouch's murder ripped back and forth across his mental. The images were so powerful and overwhelming that he thought that he was there all over again, with everything unfolding before his eyes. Lowering his head, he massaged the bridge of his nose and shook his head, trying to thwart off the images that poisoned his mind.

Fuller's forehead crinkled as he stared at Pavielle. "You all right, my nigga?"

"Yeah, yeah," he nodded his head somewhat convincingly. Placing his fist to his mouth, he coughed and focused back on the photos. "Which one of these fools was the one leading this execution?"

"This one," he pointed to the photo of Fernando 'Chop' Ruiz, tapping his finger against it. He'd never forget that mothafucka's face. He was stabbing Gouch so viciously that you would have thought that he'd owed him money.

"You sure?" Pavielle picked up the photo of Chop and studied his scowling face.

"Yeah, I'm fa sho'." he rubbed his hands together, staring at the photograph himself.

"Alright, this one right here," he slightly shook the photo. "I don't want homie touched. Nah, I want his ass alive and breathing."

Fuller's face balled up and he looked at him like he wasn't making any sense at all. "Fuck you wanna keep this nigga alive for?"

"Somebody hadda hire this mothafucka, and I want the nigga that put the battery into his back. That's the cock sucka that ordered the hit, and that's the nigga that's gone feel my pain." his eyebrows arched and his nose scrunched up. He tightened his jaws and the bone structure appeared in them.

"Alright." he nodded his understanding. "The rest of these niggaz are me and my guys to deal with, right?"

"Fa sho, I just want 'em gone."

"I gotchu."

"How many of yo' dudes you bringing in on this? I don't want too many heads on this thing, you Griff me?"

"Yeah, whatever the fuck that means." Fuller told him. "It will be just me, Savoy, Chambers, Dinkle and Ironside."

"That's what? Five mothafuckaz? Alright, bool, how much they won't in they bags?"

"Fiddy a piece."

"Fifty grand a piece? Alright, I can fade that."

"Yezzir, that's what I'm talking about." He smiled and rubbed his hands together greedily.

"This the deal, homie, half up front and I'll kick in the other half after the job is done."

"No problem. When you kicking out that down payment?"

"Tonight. Now, when can you tighten these eses up?"

"Consider them already gone."

"I like how you do business," Pavielle nodded. "Remember, this nigga right here," he held up Chop's photo.

"You keep him alive for me. I'ma needa bleed this dick sucka for some intell'."

"My nigga, don't worry about nothing, I got chu." he pounded his fist to his chest.

"Good." he passed him back the photograph and patted him on his back, as he trekked back towards the Escalade.

Chapter Six

Pavielle hopped into the front passenger seat of the Escalade and slammed the door shut. He pulled a lighter out of his pocket and took the roach end of a blunt out from the ashtray.

"Yo, we good?" Banga asked, firing up the truck so that they could pull off. He'd just glanced up to see that nigga Fuller pulling off too.

"Ummmm, hmmmm," he replied, lighting up the roach and expelling smoke. He quickly cracked the window and fanned away the cloud that he'd created. "Nigga said he gone take care of 'em pronto. All I gotta do is sit back and wait for the call."

"Bool," Killa Dre said from the backseat.

"Fucking May Mays peeled the homie, they gotta feel it." Banga added, eyebrows arched and jaws clenched.

"You mothafucking right," Pavielle agreed.

He focused his attention out of the passenger side window, thinking about all his life how he'd been surrounded by death. It tripped him out how it was a part of the lifestyle he'd chosen to live. He recalled the first time he killed someone. He'd remembered it like it was his last name.

Flashback

Pavielle and Gouch sat low in the backseat of Bully's dull black 1967 Chevy Impala. Bully captained the low-rider while Gangsta road shotgun. Ragtop up, the foursome coasted through enemy territory looking for some crips to blast on. The O.Gs put a sherm stick into rotation. Everyone on board the old school classic took a hit of the dipped cigarette, even Pavielle. The young nigga was hesitant at first but Bully told him it would help him in his mission. Pavielle took a few pulls of the funny cigarette and before long he was feeling its full effects. It was a high he had never experienced before, far greater than weed. He felt invincible, like he could take on a million crips and win. He looked over to Gouch and could tell the sherm had him feeling the same way.

"Ya'll good back there?" Bully asked, looking at the boys through the rearview mirror.

"Two sho, big homie," Pavielle replied, "Just anxious to find these crabs and smoke 'em."

"Show y'all how us young niggaz get down." Gouch said, giving his baby brother dap. "I don't give a fuck if a nigga grand momma is outside, her old ass can get it, too!"

"Them young niggaz are feeling that water, blood. They're on one." Bully smiled proudly, looking back and forth between the windshield and Gangsta.

"Yeah," Gangsta managed a weak smile. *He still wasn't feeling letting his nephews join the set, but whether he agreed with it or not, eventually they were going to get put on. It was just a matter of time. At least this way he'd be there to make sure everything went smoothly.*

"What's up with chu, bomrade? As much work as we done put in together I know you don't have butterflies?" Bully frowned.

"Nah, I'm good," Gangsta replied, taking a swallow of Hennessy from the bottle. He passed it off to Bully and he took it to the head and passed it to the backseat. Pavielle and Gouch indulged in the strong dark liquor. Their first swallows burnt their throats, but a few more swigs and they'd grown use to it. Bully took the bottle from them and passed it to Gangsta, who sat it on the floor between his knees.

"Play us some tunes, big homie." Gouch told Bully.

"What, y'all need a lil' something to put y'all in the mood?" he glanced at the youths in the backseat. *"Some of that murder music? I got just the theme."* He said, sliding a disc into the Alpine stereo. He skipped through the tracks until

he found the one he was looking for. A moment later Spice 1's Born II Die came pumping through the Chevy's speakers. Pavielle and Gouch nodded their heads to the infectious tunes, mentally preparing themselves for the murders they were about to commit. Gangsta nodded his head to the beat and stroked the Uzi resting in his lap as if it were a Persian feline.

From behind the lenses of his shades, Bully spotted a crowd of crips posted up in front of a peach apartment building. He quickly executed the headlights of the Impala and turned off the Alpine stereo.

"Aye, blood, what's up?" *Pavielle whispered, wondering why Bully stopped the music.*

"Shhhh," *Bully responded with a finger to his lips. He pointed to the windshield at the crips hanging out in front of the apartment building.* "There them niggaz go, slipping like a bad transmission."

Bully pulled the old school six houses down and across the street from the apartment building the crips were posted out in front of. He executed the Impala's engine and turned around to address Pavielle and Gouch. "Alright," *He began.* "Y'all lil' niggaz hop out and do y'all thang. Me and Gangsta gone post right here."

Pavielle and Gouch spilled out into the street where their unsuspecting targets wouldn't detect them. bangers at their sides, the brothers moved in on the apartments under the camouflage of the night. They used the parked cars lined up on the block to their advantage, taking cover behind them as they moved along. They took refuge behind an old navy blue van, which was about ten feet away from the apartments. The crips were oblivious to their enemies' presence. They were too busy smoking, drinking and filling each other in on the latest hood gossip.

"Nigga, guess who I dicked down last night," a tall, big head dude wearing a black beanie and brown Dickie suit said, passing a 40 .oz of Olde English to his homeboy standing next to him.

"Who?" a skinny youth in a Orlando Magics jersey asked, throwing his head back and blowing smoke into the air from the joint he held between his bony fingers.

"Shaniqua, nigga, I was all in that bitch guts; wearing it out." Dickie suit claimed, hands outstretched as he humped the air.

"Why you lying on your dick, nigga?" a brown skinned kid rocking a flat-top with a hook in it asked. "That *broad got locked up the day before yesterday for boosting clothes outta the Slauson."*

All of the homies gathered spat out there alcohol or choked on their smoke, laughing. Brown Dickie suit wore a dumbfounded expression on his face.

"Cuz, always lying on his dick," Flat-top snickered and slapped hands with another one of their homeboys.

Pavielle and Gouch gave each other a nod before spinning from behind the van, guns blazing. Flames and smoke roared from the barrels of the brothers' weapons as they engaged their enemies. The crips scrambled, screamed and hollered as their warm flesh met with hot lead. All they saw were the muzzle flashes that gave them brief glimpses of their assailants' faces. After laying down four of the six crips, Pavielle and Gouch ascended on the last two that had broke for the building's entrance. Dickie suit cleared the threshold into the apartment building before Magics jersey could. He slammed the door on him and left him as food for the young wolves. Left out in the cold, Magics jersey banged on the door and pleaded for his homeboy to let him in, but his calls were ignored. Dickie suit had already locked the door and ascended up the staircase.

A sharp whistle grabbed the crip's attention from the door. He whipped around and found the murderous scowls of the hooded killers. The way the two were staring him down he thought their beef may have been personal, but after running their faces through his mental rolodex he came to the conclusion that he had never met the duo before.

"What the fuck y'all want from me, cuz?" *Magics jersey asked, his voice cracking under fear. His eyes were as big as saucers and his chest was jumping from his raging heart.*

"Your life mothafucka," *Gouch roared. He and Pavielle pulled the triggers of their bangers, muzzle flashes lighting up the night. Their weapons recoiled in their palms as they let off rounds. Bullets tore through Magics jersey's torso, exited his back, and struck the glass door of the complex's entrance. The glass was cracked into several spider cobwebs and stained with blood. Magics jersey slammed into the door, hit the ground and rolled over onto his side, eyes staring out of their corners at nothing. Gouch and Pavielle kicked the front door of the apartment building open and rushed inside towards the staircase.*

***

"Them lil' dudes ain't playing," Bully told Gangsta after seeing Pavielle and Gouch gundown Magics jersey in the entrance of the building, "They young ridaz with it."

"The blood of warriors' courses through these veins," Gangsta swept his gloved hand over the veins of his arm.

"Is that, right?" Bully smirked. The expression quickly faded when he saw something through the windshield. He hurriedly resurrected the engine and pulled from the curb.

"What's up?" Gangsta asked concerned, sitting up in his seat.

Bully gripped his Uzi with one hand and steered the Chevy with the other. "Grab your tool, blood. Some of these niggaz still kicking."

***

Dickie suit ran through the hallway of the 2nd floor pounding on residing residents' doors, pleading for them to let him in. Realizing that no one was going to oblige him, he gave up and jogged down the corridor, taking brief glances over his shoulder. When he looked ahead he found the shorter of the two killers reaching the top step. Spooked, he turned around on his heels and hauled ass in the opposite direction. As soon as he bent the corner at the end of the corridor, his chest was greeted with three bursts from Gouch's .45 automatic. His *face twisted into a mask of excruciation, as if he'd caught a whiff of some funky ass pussy.*

Blood streamed from the black holes in Dickie suit's body as he lay on his back. Tears ran free from his eyes as he whimpered and coughed up blood. Seeing The Grim Reaper in the form of Gouch standing over him with an automatic handgun pointed between his eyes, caused him to tremble uncontrollably. Terrified, he pleaded for his momma to come and save him from the nightmare that was to be his end.

Click!

"Fuck!" Gouch cursed. He checked the magazine of his weapon and it was empty.

Pavielle brushed his brother aside and finished off Dickie suit with two rounds to the skull. For a time the youth stood there studying the expression on his victim's face, observing the blood pooling beneath his head. Dead bodies were nothing new to him. He'd seen plenty in his young life but this was the first one he'd created.

"Come on!" Gouch pulled Pavielle along.

Together, they took off running, their sneakers screeching on the scuffed, shiny floor.

***

Screeeeech!

The Chevy came to a halt outside of the apartment building. Bully and Gangsta hopped out with firm grips on their Uzis. They ran upon the few bloody and squirming crips that were on the ground, squeezing their triggers. Their automatic weapons rattled to life and vibrated in their palms as they spat rapid fire tearing holes into their targets domes and backs, misting the air with shallow sprays of blood.

"Y'all come on!" Gangsta waved his nephews on when they spilled out of the building. Pavielle and Gouch slid into the backseat of the old school and slammed the door closed. The Chevy pulled away from the murder scene with police sirens wailing in the distance.

***

Birdman hoisted his slender frame upon the tarred roof of his apartment building. After dusting himself off, he made a beeline over to the pigeon coop. The coop was shelter for a total of thirty-five pigeons; all varying in different sizes and colors. Black, white, brown and gray were just some of the shades of the feathered creatures. The pigeons were flapping around wildly inside of the coop when their keeper approached; it wasn't until Birdman leaned forward and communicated to them in their language that they all settled down. *"Coo! Coo! Coo!"* Birdman made the noises his feathered friends make, mimicking their head movements.

The pigeons seemed to be listening as their keeper interacted with them; it was as if the creatures could understand him. Birdman paused and waited for the pigeons' response, listening closely as the birds replied.

"Coo! Coo! Coo!" The pigeons answered back.

Birdman uttered one more Coo, and the way it rolled off of his tongue, it was as if he was saying *"thank you"* to the birds. Birdman produced a key from his pocket and unlocked the door of the coop. Once he opened the door, he stood to the side of the coop and clapped in a sporadic rhythm, all the while mimicking the pigeons' neck movements and uttering Coos. The pigeons flapped around wildly inside of the coop and then they took off, soaring across the moonlit sky.

The Birdman had gotten his name for his love of birds. He had raised over forty pigeons. Though he was a blood, he never carried any kind of weapon. It was rumored that he had trained his pigeons so well that they'd attack an enemy on command.

***

Monk stood on the porch of his home holding a bottle of Hennessy. There were homeboys and homegirls from the set from his generation and the next on either side of him. They were all staring up into the sky waiting for a sign.

Once Pavielle and Gouch's mission was successfully carried out, Bully was to put in a call to Birdman and let him know that everything had gone as planned. Birdman was to then release a flock of pigeons that were to fly north, confirming the boys' passage into the gang.

Birdman's pigeons flew above every ones head and over Monk's house. A broad smile stretched across Monk's lips. All the homeboys and homegirls from the set went wild whistling, cheering and jumping up and down. Some of them even took to the dirt patched lawn to do the Blood Walk.

***

As soon as Bully and the gang hopped out of his Chevy they were greeted by the aroma of weed and the sounds of I get around by Digital Underground, both of which were flowing from the cracked windows of Monk's home. The homeboys and homegirls had brought the celebration from the front lawn to the living room of Monk's place. The function taking place inside of the yellow and brown house was as live as a Prince concert.

Pavielle and Gouch hopped out of the car and bolted towards the steps, before they could reach the front door Monk came staggering out, as drunk as a sailor.

"Y'all made it!" He said, opening his arm to receive them. "Welcome to the family!"

Pavielle and Gouch exchanged glances and smiled at Monk. They could tell that he was drunk and high, which wasn't out of the ordinary for him. Since the day he lost his left-arm from the spray of an AK-47 during a drive by, Monk, or The One Arm Monk as the homies referred to him stayed getting lit.

"Fuck y'all waiting for?" Monk asked, wondering why the boys he considered his nephews hadn't embraced him yet. "Y'all too gangsta to show your uncle some love? Say it ain't so."

The brothers embraced Monk.

"Y'all straight, y'all alright?" he gave the boys the once over. They nodded yes. "Did your uncle bless y'all with names yet?"

"Yeah," Pavielle spoke up for the first time. "We just kept our nick names. Gucci is still Gouch and I'm still Booby, but only I added a loc to it. You know, like Booby Loc?"

"Loc?" Monk said, twisting his face. "Loc is some crab shit, that's their thing."

"Nah, not like that," Pavielle said. "Like loco, like I'm crazy, Y.G Booby Loco. That's my hood name."

"Alright then," Monk ruffled Pavielle's head and threw his arm over Gouch's shoulders. "Y'all come on; I'm drunk and high and gotta find something to put my third leg in tonight."

When Monk ushered Pavielle and Gouch through the door of his home, he called for everyone in the living room attention. Seeing that he had every ones attention, he introduced them to the newest additions to their set: Y.G Gouch and Y.G Booby Loco. Pavielle and Gouch were greeted by homeboys and homegirls of the Eastside 20s republic; most of them they knew while others were only vaguely familiar to them.

Gangsta caught Pavielle eying one of the homegirls from the hood; she was sitting on the couch with a few other girls from the neighborhood. Her name was China Doll. China Doll was what you would call ghetto fine. She was high-yellow with long silky black hair, which she kept in a ponytail that reached her perfectly round ass. She had slanted eyes and full lips that glistened with MAC lip gloss. There was *a stud piercing right below them. Her B-cup breasts, though small, matched perfectly with her curvaceous, hippy frame.*

"You see something you like?" Gangsta nodded towards the living room couch, occupied by a handful of homegirls.

"Ah, nah," Pavielle waved the homegirls off. "I'm not thinking about them hoes."

"What?" Gangsta snapped, not believing what his nephew said. "Don't tell me you're scared of some pussy, man." He leaned in close enough for Pavielle to smell the liquor on his hot breath, and then asked. "You fucking yet, Booby?"

"Come on now, unc," Pavielle blushed and shamefully hung his head, waving his uncle off. "You know me."

"Come on now, unc, you know me!" Gangsta mocked his nephew. "Coldblooded killer, and he ain't never had no pussy. Ain't no virgins from the hood so we're about to dead that shit right now." The O.G threw his arm over his youngest nephew's shoulders. "It's alright, nephew, ain't nothing to be embarrassed about. Shit, if you haven't had no pussy before, then I know Gucci hasn't either. You two niggaz are birds of a feather."

Gangsta called for Gouch, who was in the kitchen on his knees shooting craps. Hearing his uncle call for him, he scooped up his money and handed one of the Y.Gs the dice he was rolling with. He then made his way into the living room where his uncle and brother were. Gangsta took Gouch under his other arm and pulled him in closer. "Y'all gone and take y'all pick." He told his nephews, referring to the homegirls on the living room couch.

Pavielle pointed out China Doll and Gouch opted for Thangz. Thangz was a petite brown skinned girl with short hair that came just past her ear. She had a nose-ring and a diamond belly piercing, but her ass was as flat as an Asian girl's. But for what Thangz lacked in the rear, she more than made up for with her 36 double D bust-line. Her big breasts were the soul reason the O.Gs christened her "Thangz". The first thing people would say when they laid eyes on her was, 'Damn, look at those big old thangz!'

"Alright," Gangsta said, rubbing his hands together. "Let me work my magic."

Gangsta left the boys to themselves while he went to go holler at the girls they had requested. Pavielle and Gouch looked on as their uncle conversed with the girls they had picked out. Moments later, Gangsta returned with a shit-eating-grin on his face.

"They with it," He told his nephews, handing them a condom each.

The boys stuffed the condoms into their pockets. Gangsta dapped up his nephews before making his exit. China Doll took Pavielle by the hand and led him into the bedroom down the hall, while Thangz took Gouch and lead him into the bathroom.

***

"So," China Doll began, unbuckling Pavielle's pants, "is this your first time?"

Paville nodded yes. "A virgin, huh? I'm about to get your young ass sprung off this pussy." She claimed.

Watching China Doll undo his pants, Pavielle's heart was beating almost as fast as it was when he and Gouch blasted on the crips earlier that night. The blood in his scrawny frame flowed like pouring springs and rushed through the shaft of his dick. The way his fuck-muscle slowly gave to an erection, it was as if it was being inflated. China Doll was impressed by the size of the Y.G's manhood. The little nigga was holding to only be twelve years old. The youngster meat was as hard as a stick of dynamite.

As soon as China Doll took Pavielle into her warm, wet mouth, his eyes doubled in size and he clenched his ass cheeks together. Once she got to bobbing up and down his shaft, all of his pent up anxiety vanished.

"Oh, shit!" Pavielle cursed, his eyes rolled to the back of his head and he stood on the tips of his toes.

China Doll was sucking his dick as if it were a Popsicle melting under the warmth of the sun on a ninety degree day. Pavielle tried to grab her by the back of her head so that he could fuck her mouth, like he once saw a stud do in a porno but she smacked his hand away. China Doll continued to handle her business until she felt her fuck-buddy's dick nudging the back of her throat. Knowing he was about to bust, she pulled away and stood to her feet.

"What chu stop for?" Pavielle frowned. He wanted that nut badly.

China Doll didn't say a word; she disrobed and took the condom from Pavielle's pocket. She tore the wrapper open with her teeth, removed the greasy latex rubber and slid it down Pavielle's shaft until she reached his pubic hairs. She then crawled upon the bed, laid on her back and opened her legs to a fat pussy with a strip of hair, as silky as the ones gracing her crown. She then took two fingers, parted her *pussy lips and massaged herself. She moaned in ecstasy as her walls gave way to wetness, her nectar oozing from between her thighs and soiling the sheets.*

"Are you gone come get this pussy or what?" She asked Pavielle between moans. Little momma was hot, on fire, and she wanted his young ass up in her.

Pavielle kicked off his pants and hurried out of his hoodie. After abandoning his garments on the nappy carpet, he crawled upon the bed where China Doll took him by his dick, guiding him into her tunnel of pleasure. A chill snaked its way up his spine as soon as he entered her. His eyes rolled to their whites and his mouth involuntarily opened. He couldn't believe how good she felt.

After she gave him instructions on how to fuck her, Pavielle began to work himself in and out of her womb at a slow, steady pace. China Doll let go of a soft moan, licking her lips and biting down on the bottom one. Pavielle was now moving faster between her legs, grunting and cursing under his breath. It wasn't long before he was shiny all over from sweat and his heart was booming behind his chest. Feeling his dick head tingling, he sped up a notch. China Doll pulled the sheets and screamed like the young Outlaw was laying it down, but it was only to stroke his ego. Thirty seconds later,

Pavielle busted into the condom and collapsed onto her small breasts. He lied on top of China Doll, heart pounding and panting out of breath. He was sweat and sticky, but she didn't mind. China Doll smirked, kissing him on the top of his head and caressing the side of his face as he lay against her.

***

Thangz was lying face down with her ass up on the bathroom floor; Gouch was behind her pounding away. The young nigga's body glistened with sweat as he worked his way toward a nut to bust on Thangz flat ass. She hollered out in ecstasy and her eyes rolled to the back of her head, hearing his pelvis smack up against her rear. Gouch was laying his dick game down like a pro.

Contrary to Gangsta's beliefs, Gouch was not a virgin. He had popped his cherry a year earlier. A smoker by the name of Mousey had an arrangement with him; she would give him some ass and a shot of head for a twenty dollar fix. Mousey hadn't been addict to crack cocaine that long. So she still possessed a fairly decent body. The only drawback was the top row of teeth she was missing thanks to her crack head, pimp of a boyfriend, Fatso, punching her in the mouth. But Gouch found a way around that, he would only smash her from the back. Those were the good old days for Gouch; sadly all good things must come to an end.

Old Mousey got knocked on a murder charge and was sent up north. She had grown sick and tired of Fatso beating her up and taking the crack she had worked so hard for and smoking it all himself. Fed up, the one hundred pound crack whore withdrew a pair of scissors from her purse and drove it through the fat bastard's heart. Fatso dropped dead on the spot, right on the corner of 47th and Avalon. Mousey snatched the crack rocks from the overweight pimp's meaty palm, sat on his gut, and smoked it. By the time the police showed up, she was too spaced out to make a run for it. She didn't even put up a fight when they clamped the metal bracelets around her wrists and shoved her into the back of a squad car. It had been a while since Gouch got himself a piece, and he promised himself that he was going to knock the pussy lining out of his next sex partner. And so here he was, pumping and sweating.

"Ah, fuck," Gouch shouted, gripping Thangz naked hips. "Here it comes!"

"Give it to me, baby!" Thangz shouted. "Oh, I want chu to bust all over my ass!"

"Here it goes!" Gouch gritted, hopping to his feet and pulling off the rubber. He jacked himself off and droplets of semen rained upon Thangz ass as she shook it. She smiled happily, shaking her buttocks continuously.

"You sure you were a virgin?" Thangz asked, wiping the semen from her ass with toilet paper.

"Yeah," Gouch said, trying to refrain from laughing while he zipped and buttoned up his Levi's.

"Well, I ain't ever met a virgin that fucked like that!" Thangz said, putting her clothes back on.

Gouch smiled mischievously.

***

That night Gouch and Pavielle lied in their twin beds, neither one of them could fall asleep. Gouch stared up at the ceiling while Pavielle tossed and turned. Giving up his quest for dream world, Pavielle turned over in bed towards Gouch.

"Gouch?"

"What?"

"Are you asleep?"

"Nah?"

"How come?"

"Shit, I don't know. I just can't sleep."

"I can't sleep either," Pavielle admitted. "I keep seeing that boy's face and hearing him begging for his momma."

Gouch turned over in bed towards Pavielle, propping his fist against the side of his head. "What boy?

Pavielle looked around the bedroom as if to make sure no one was around to hear him before answering. "That last boy I smoked back at the apartments."

"Blood went out like a bitch." Gouch snickered.

"Did you see him or any of the other crabs we smoked when you close your eyes?"

"Man, hell naw!" Gouch said. "Fuck them niggaz, this bloods!" he threw up the blood gang sign.

"How did you feel after we killed them fools?"

"Nothing; numb," Gouch admitted, shrugging his shoulders. "Why? You regretting smoking them bustas now?"

"Nah, like you said, 'fuck them niggaz!' They were caught slipping and they got what they deserved," Pavielle proclaimed. "Besides, we had to do what we had to do to protect the hood, right?"

"You're damn right!"

"I just wish old boy would go away," Pavielle said, lying back in bed and taking a deep breath. Seeing the crip's face that he killed had him afraid to go to sleep. "I'm tired of seeing his dumb ass face and hearing his dumb ass voice every time I close my eyes."

"It's all up here!" Gouch said, pointing to his temple. "That's your enemy's only way of attacking you now. Mothafucka can't get chu in the physical, so he's going at your mental." Gouch snuggled under the covers and turned on his side to try to get some sleep. "Don't worry about that fool, though, Booby," he shut his eyes. "He'll go away."

"Oh, yeah? How do you know?" Pavielle asked.

"Because, if he don't stop fucking with my baby brother, I'ma smoke his ass." Gouch swore. He was as serious as a fucking heart attack too.

Pavielle snuggled under the covers and closed his eyes to go to sleep, Moments later, he drifted off to sleep with a smirk on his face. He was happy to have a brother that would kill to protect him. He felt like the luckiest kid in the world. He knew Gouch was as down for him as much as he was down for Gouch. They were blood brothers as well as best friends. Pavielle didn't get any more visits from the boy he had murdered that night and he believed it was because the boy feared he might run into his big brother Gouch.

Present

Pavielle dapped up Killa Dre and Banga, bidding them a farewell as he strode into the yard. He threw his head back like *What's up?* To Tay and Mad Man, who were posted on the porch, passing a blunt between them. They invited Pavielle to smoke with them. And although he wasn't in the mood, he didn't want to be rude so he took a few drags and kicked the shit with them for a time. Afterwards, he ducked off inside of the house where he found his family asleep. He got undressed and took a shower. Once he was done, he threw on some boxer briefs and carried his gun over to the side where he slept. He stashed his banger underneath his pillow and slid under the sheets, kissing his family goodnight as they slept peacefully.

Staring up at the ceiling with his hands clasped at the back of his head, Pavielle couldn't believe all of the trouble that came with being Top Dawg. I mean, sure it had its benefits, but goddamn, was it really worth him losing so many people that he loved? To him it was funny when people said that if they could go back in time and change their life they wouldn't, because at this very moment, if he could, he would have never become a gangsta. Fuck the hood, fuck his gang, his money, fuck bitches, fuck crack and fuck boss status. He'd give all of that shit up just to see all of his loved ones again.

Thinking about his loved ones caused Pavielle's eyes to well up with tears. He bit down on his bottom lip and tears jetted down his cheeks. He made an ugly ass face and broke down sobbing, turning on his side and punching the mattress. His tears flew off the side and soiled the bed sheet. He gritted and tried to keep quiet, but eventually his making noise awoke Vayda. She turned over in bed with furrowed brows, wondering what was troubling her man.

"Baby, what's wrong?" she asked concerned, rubbing his arm soothingly as he lay on his side.

"It's my fault, Vay. It's all my fault," he kept saying between sobs, snot threatening to drip.

"What's your fault, bae? Talk to me." She urged him.

"It's 'cause of me that everyone is dead," his voice cracked under his emotions. His heart was heavy with grief.

"What are you talking about?" her forehead creased.

Pavielle turned around in bed, sniffling and looking up into her eyes.

"G-momma, Gangsta, Gouch, Rydah Man, Debo, Woo, Big Head, Panic, all the rest of the homies, are dead 'cause of me," he believed. "It's 'cause of my selfish, bullheaded ass that they're all dead! Me, it's my fucking fault!" he bawled like he was his newborn son in the middle of the night.

"Shhhhhh! That's nonsense, come here," she pulled him into her, resting his head against her breasts. This was comforting to him. She was warm and he could feel her heart beating. It had a steady beat pattern. She gentle caressed the side of his head. "Them being dead isn't your fault, Pavy. It was just their time. Like one day, it'll be my time and your time. All you and I can do is make the best out of the time we have while we're here." She continued to caress the side of his head as he lay against her breasts, listening to her heart beat. He was staring up at her, looking peaceful and calm. That's when she began to sing. Her astonishing voice sounded like a choir of angels crooning and stroking the delicate strings of a violin. Her vocals carried him off to a utopia all his own, and before she knew it, he'd fallen asleep in her arms. Shortly, she was following right behind him.

    There's nothing like the love of a good woman.

Chapter Seven

The next day

Midget turned off the dials of the shower head and walked his naked brown ass over to the lockers to get dressed. Before he knew it four skinheads rushed in with sharpened steel, his eyes bulged and he gasped. He turned to run away but was quickly overwhelmed. He howled in agony as the prison made shanks pierced every inch of his body. All of the racist bastards treated his strewn form like a pincushion. He threw up his arms and legs to shield himself from the assault but this did little help. Midget pissed on himself he was so terrified of having his life taken. The grunts of the Aryans filled the air as they stabbed at his form, seven inch blades penetrating his warm flesh. Each stab caused blood to fly everywhere. Speckles of plasma clung to the killers' faces and half naked bodies. Even after the little man lay lifeless they were still hacking away at his limp form. He slightly jerked as the steel was plunged into him and yanked out of him. His eyes were staring up at the ceiling at nothing and his mouth was ajar, tongue slightly visible at the corner of his lips. Having finished the job that they were paid for, the skinheads stood erect and took the time to admire their handiwork. The leader of their pack wiped their victim's specks of blood from off his face with the hand that clutched his shank. His, as well as the rest of his gangs' chests, jumped fast from their pounding hearts. Satisfied, they washed the blood from off them and their weapons before leaving the shower room. Once they'd abandoned the shower room, Fuller peeked inside from the entrance to make sure that the deed was done. A sinister smile curled his lips and he walked off whistling Dixie.

Midget lay lifeless with the showerhead water beating down on his body and rinsing the blood off him. The blood mixed with the water and turned it pink.

Meanwhile

The mess hall was a mesh of inmates indulging in conversation and laughter. Everyone was carrying on as if they didn't have a care in the world but this couldn't even be further from the truth. See, they were well aware that they were in county jail, and never knew when some shit was going to crack off. So they had to make sure that they were on point at all times. It was either that or get caught slipping.

Nino sat at his table with the rest of his homeboys enjoying his meal. For the past couple of minutes he had been stuffing his face with what appeared to be stew. It tasted like shit, but he found out that with a little salt the dish wasn't that bad. Nino had just swallowed some of the stew when his eyes bulged and his mouth flew open. Suddenly, he regurgitated some of the stew, spitting it up. The last of it came flooding down his chin and soiling his uniform. His eyes turned glassy and he gagged, veins etching up his temples. His behavior caused all of his niggaz to look at him with worried expressions on their faces. The collective of them kept asking him what was wrong, but he didn't answer because he was all choked up.

Nino shot to his feet and held his stomach. He took off running across the mess hall as fast as he could, hollering and coughing up his lunch. He suddenly tripped and fell. Turning to his right, he fell on his side and clutched his stomach. He grimaced, slobber and stew spilling out of his mouth. He bawled and turned on his side, feeling the sickest he'd ever been in his life.

"Arrrrrrghhhh!" he gritted, blinking his eyelids rapidly. His performance drew the stares and the assistance of other inmates that were wondering what the fuck was going on with him. "Help, help, somebody...gaaaaa....ahhhhh!" he gritted harder and pressed his head back against the floor, lifting his back up off the surface. He pressed the tips of his shoes against the floor and lifted his ass high up in the air. Abruptly, he collapsed to the surface and fell flat out, head leaning to the side. His eyes were stretched open and so was his mouth.

Two correctional officers made their way through the crowd of on looking convicts. One of them kneeled down to Nino and touched the pulse in his neck. It was none existent. The officer looked to the other officer and shook his head, letting him know that he was dead.

The cook looked on from the kitchen where he'd seen everything go down. It was him that had poisoned the Vato's food. Just then, Officer Chambers walked up to him and slid a crisp, folded one hundred dollar bill inside of his shirt pocket. He patted him on the cheek gently and went about his business.

***

Poe Boy went down the corridor mopping the floor as he went along. He was so into the task at hand that he didn't hear an Aryan creep upon him from behind and pull a towel over his face, pulling him inside of another room. Inside there were two of his Aryan Brothers, armed with blunt objects. They rolled the mop bucket inside and shut the door behind them. A couple of the Aryan's held Poe boy's arms, while another punched his ribcage and stomped his legs until they broke. Once the cat was done beating his ass, he switched places with his comrade so he could join in on the action. By this time they'd finished, their victim was hurt so badly that he couldn't muster the strength to defend himself. Seeing this, the skinheads dropped their blunt objects and dragged him over to the mop bucket. Two of them held his arms down while the other held his face down inside of the hot murky water. The fool doing the drowning eyes took on a hateful look and he bit down hard on his bottom lip, as he held his victim underwater, watching the bubbles hastily rising to the surface. Poe Boy tried his best to get loose, but the beaten had left him weakened. He was a goner. Before long the bubbles stopped rising to the water's surface and the young Mexican man went still. With the deed done, the Aryans took the time to dry the sweat from off their faces and straighten their uniforms out before stepping out of the room. Afterwards, they went on to join the other inmates like they just didn't catch a body.

That night

Monsta rolled off of his bed and headed over to the commode, smacking his lips and rubbing his eye with a curled finger. Stopping at the toilet, he pulled out his meat and began pissing. All that could be heard was his stream of urine hitting the inside of the aluminum commode and running down inside of the toilet water. He threw his head back and licked his lips, taking a deep breath as he relieved his bladder. Hearing bare feet at his rear, he made to turned around and that's when a strong arm snaked around his forehead. The hand of the arm pressed his head back against his attacker's chest. As soon as Monsta went to make a move, heavy grunts filled his eardrums and an ice pick like shank jabbed his throat repeatedly. Blood splattered on both him and his attacker, speckling the walls and the white bed sheets.

"Gagggggg," Monsta gagged and blood drooled from the corner of his mouth. He tried to fight the son of a bitch off, but his efforts were futile. The two-hundred and fifty pound mountain of muscle was sluggish and weak from loss of blood. After a while he dropped his arms to his sides and his eyelids narrowed. He did nothing to defend himself as his attacker continued his savage assault, rapidly jabbing him in the neck with his sharpened steel. He stabbed him in the neck one last time and broke the metal off inside of his neck. Next, he released him and he fell flat on his face, busting his forehead. His face lay pressed against the cool floor and his eyes stared off at nothing, his wound pouring blood out on the surface.

The attacker dropped what was left of his weapon on the floor and sat in the corner of the cell, Indian Style. His arms were covered in blood up to his elbows and his upper half was splotched red. He shut his eyelids and formed an expressionless face, making Bs with his fingers and thumbs. He meditated and waited for the correctional officers to come to take him away.

***

Capo lie in bed fast asleep, snoring like a fat ass momma hog. One hand lay on his chest while the other was stuffed down the front of his boxers. He had been molesting his dick and balls before he fell off into a deep coma like sleep. A slot opened in the door and a substance was squirted out on his face and body. He winced and licked his lips, tasting an odd flavor.

"Gas? What the fuck?" his eyelids snapped open and he sat up in bed. A bottle of lighter fluid was pushed out through the slot. As soon as it met the floor a chubby, hairy hand emerged with a burning match pinched between its finger and thumb. Capo's eyes grew as big as golf balls and his jaw dropped. The hand flicked the match inside. It landed on his lap and he quickly went up in flames, hollering like a mothafucka. He hollered and danced all around the cell until he eventually crashed to the floor burning. The assailant hastily walked off, his bottoms smacking against the floor as he fled the scene. As soon as the alarm went off inside of the facility, the inmates went to the windows in their doors. They stared out at the cell that had the burning man in it, flames of his fire reflected in their pupils.

Soon After

Vayda lay in bed asleep behind Pavielle as he stared out of the bedroom window. He was focused on Tay and Mad Man who were posted up in front of the house chopping it up and passing a smoldering blunt between them. The young kingpin had his crying baby boy cradled in his arm, gently bouncing him.

"Shhhh, shhhh!" he hushed his little man, trying to quiet him down. He continued to bounce him and slowly his crying subsided. He looked to his face and saw that he'd just shut his eyes and he cracked a grin, kissing him on the side of his face. On the side of him lay his burnout cell phone on the nightstand. He had purchased for the sole purpose of Fuller contacting him after the hits were carried out. The burnout rang and vibrated, its screen glowing blue. He stepped over to it and picked it up. The display read as *unknown* and he answered it. He didn't say a thing; he just listened to what he was being told.

"Everything has been taken care of."

"I want confirmation."

"What kind?"

"Photos."

"No problem. I will need a few days."

"What about our other friend?"

"Bitch ass nigga is in PC, but don't worry, we'll have 'em ready for you."

"When?"

"Before dawn, I'll hit chu later with the details."

He disconnected the call.

Before dawn

The garbage truck drove through the barbwire gates of the jail and headed around back. The driver jumped down from behind the wheel and walked around to the rear of the sanitation vehicle. He gave a cautious scan of his surroundings before knocking on the enormous hatch of the transporting truck. The hatch slowly came open with a squeal revealing hordes of garbage bags and loose trash. The driver knocked on the inside of the wall of the truck in a specific pattern. Right after, Pavielle came up from the garbage dressed in a correctional officer's uniform and toting what look like a black leather bowling bag. He climbed out from where he was hidden and jumped down from out of the back of the truck, shaking the food particles from off his bag. The driver knocked on the vehicle how he did the first time and the hatch of the vehicle went to close its self. While it was performing this mechanical task, he pointed to the door that Pavielle was to enter. The young kingpin gave him a nod and went on about his business. Reaching the back door of the kitchen, he knocked on it how he was told to by the driver before making it there. He looked around to make sure that there wasn't anyone watching him as he listened to the locks of the door being undone. There was a strange sound as a latch was lifted off the iron door and it was opened. Pavielle came face to face with a white correctional officer. He handed him the bag and crossed the threshold into the facility. The correctional officer shut the door behind him and peered inside of the bag while Pavielle gave a good look around the kitchen. There wasn't a soul in sight.

The officer smiled with satisfaction seeing all of the dead presidents inside of the bag. He stashed his pay off inside of the freezer and accompanied Pavielle on a walk down a long corridor. The men wore serious expressions along their journey, giving nods to the staff that they came across in the hallway. The officer took Pavielle on the segregation unit where they housed the unruly inmates; this is where he would find Chop awaiting him. Coming down the walkway, Pavielle slid on a pair of black leather gloves, flexing his fingers in them and pulling them down on his hands. Up ahead, he spotted two other correctional officers. They gave him a nod as he approached, returning the gesture. Once they stopped at the door that the intended victim was in, Fuller tapped him and handed him a bowie knife. He took it and stood aside as one of the other officers opened the door for him, lifting the latch and pulling it ajar. As soon as he crossed the threshold he found Chop in his boxers blindfolded. His wrists and ankles were tied up to the corners of the bed and his mouth was gagged with one of his socks, with duct-tape lying over it.

    Pavielle sat beside him on the bed, looking him over, as the correctional officers stood outside of the door. They were to act as lookouts while the young kingpin laid down his murder game.

    Pavielle ripped the duct-tape off dude's lips and snatched the sock out of his mouth, tossing it aside.

    "Who's...Who's there?"Chop stammered as he lay in bed shiny from sweat and trembling all over, uncontrollably.

He knew something bad was going to happen to him, he just didn't know what. If he was going to be killed then he hoped his death would be quick and painless. But given the circumstances he felt like he wouldn't have such luck.

"Death," Pavielle spoke in a frightening voice. His hushed tone caused his victim to tremble that much harder. He smiled evilly and licked his lips. Next, he pricked his finger with the tip of the knife and a dot of blood appeared. He sucked the blood from off his finger. As soon as he pressed his knife into Chop's peck it startled him. He watched as beads of sweat ran down his forehead, and he swallowed the ball of nervousness in his throat, not knowing what to expect. Feeling the tip of the blade traveling down his torso, Chop lifted his head off the pillow like he could see what was going on. Unfortunately, this was impossible being he was still blindfolded. He bit down hard on his bottom lip, feeling like he was about to have his manhood severed.

"Oh, God, oh, God, please…" he begged, the bitch bleeding up out of him.

"Oh you wanna turn religious now, huh? You wasn't all that sanctified when you murked my brotha." Pavielle's forehead furrowed.

"Yo' hermano?"

"Yes, my mothafucking brotha," he removed his blindfold so that he could see his face. Pavielle's eyes were pink and running with tears, thinking of how Gouch had been done by the Mexicans. Scenes of his horrific murder played inside of his head like a movie at a theater. Seeing this all over again enraged him and he became thirsty for the blood of his brother's killer.

When Chop saw Pavielle's face he nearly shit himself. He remembered his face that day when he and his homeboys butchered his brother and threw him over the guard railing. His voice echoed over and over again inside of his head.

"You're dead, you hear me? Every last one of you bitches are dead, count on it!"

With murder on his brain, Pavielle straddled Chop and punched him in the face twice, bloodying his grill. His teeth and his mouth was coated red with blood. Wincing, the Vato turned his head trying to avoid another blow to the face. Pavielle grabbed his ho ass by his throat, causing him to choke and his eyes to bulge. He blinked his eyelids rapidly and moisture built up in them.

"Gaaaaaa," He gagged and wheezed out of breath.

"Listen, cock sucka," Pavielle began, gritting his teeth. "I wanna know who put chu and yo' faggot ass homeboys up to knocking off my brotha. I'ma ask you that one mothafucking time, and if I even think you lying, I'm jamming my friend here up yo' asshole." He held up the bowie knife and a gleam swept up the length of it. "You Griff me?"

"Wha…what?" Chop asked hoarsely.

"You feel me?"

"Ye…Yes."

"Alright then," As Pavielle listened to what he was being told, his forehead wrinkled with lines. He couldn't believe that the nigga that ordered his brother's murder had been under his nose the entire time. His eyes widen and his jaw dropped. He looked over his shoulder at Fuller and the rest of the correctional officers. They shrugged not knowing what he expected them to do. Pavielle set his sights back on Chop and crammed his sock into his mouth, taping it back over his lips. Gripping his knife with both hands, he slammed it through his victim's chest, hearing it meet bone. The first strike caused his eyes to bug and he struggled to get loose, but his efforts were futile. The stabs behind the first one came swift and without mercy, splattering blood everywhere. Speckles of blood clung to the side of the wall, Chop, Pavielle's uniform and his face. He looked like a mad man, as he continued to stab the already dead man, making a mess. Chop's body jerked violently as it was repeatedly assaulted. The correctional officers cringed and turned their heads away from the gruesome sight, not being able to stomach the grotesque sight before their eyes.

Pavielle fell on top of his victim breathing hard, having exhausted himself from all of that stabbing. After a while, he sat up and climbed off the corpse that he had created. He wiped his face with the back of his gloved hand and smeared the blood that was already there. As he headed to the door, the C.Os looked at him like he had lost his mothafucking mind.

"Damn, this shit is all over my face, ain't it?" he asked Fuller.

"Yeah."

"You got something I can clean myself off with."

Fuller nodded and pulled a rag from his back pocket, passing it to him. He and the other officers watched Pavielle wipe his face clean and try to hand the rag back. Fuller declined and insisted that he keep it.

Pavielle stuffed the rag into his back pocket and went on to address Fuller. "You heard that name back there? I want that nigga'z address, ASAP. I also want the pictures that confirm the deaths of those other five Mexicans."

"Don't worry about nothing, big dawg. I got chu faded." Fuller assured him, taking the knife from him with a handkerchief.

Pavielle left the jail feeling a little better having just killed off the last man that had stabbed up Gouch. He was one step closer to getting the man that ordered the hit on his brother.

***

It was dawn by the time Pavielle came strolling out of the back door of the kitchen. He moved about casually, like he just didn't finish stabbing a nigga to death. He climbed inside of the back of the garbage truck and waited until he was concealed inside. After putting a surgical mask over his nose and mouth, he sat down on the garbage and folded his arms across his chest. Feeling the truck shake as it was brought back to life by its driver; he laid his head back and shut his eyelids. He couldn't believe the name that Chop had dropped on him. Out of all of the men that had could have ordered Gouch's execution, it was the one that he least expected. No matter how hard he tried to put together a motive for the suspect in question, he couldn't come up with one for shit. Although Chop could have been lying, he had a strong feeling that he wasn't, especially with how scary his ass was talking.

Nah, that nigga Chop was definitely telling the truth, because he didn't have a reason to lie. He may not have known the nigga'z reasoning for putting a hit on Gouch, but one goddamn thing was for sure: he was going to find out before he slit his throat from ear to ear.

Chapter Eight

That day

Killa Dre looked alive and tapped the windshield when he saw a gray Cutlass pull inside of the parking lot bumping Do or Die's *'Po Pimp'*. This was to alert Banga to the presence of the fools that they were supposed to be meeting there. Instantly, Banga hopped out of the ride and slammed the door shut, coming to stand beside his man. Together, they watched the limo tinted Cutlass drive inside of the lot, searching for the right spot to park. That thang was sitting on '22 inch rims which casted a rainbow from the sunlight shining on them. The car parked two vehicles down from Killa Dre and Banga. Two niggaz hopped out, looking thugged the fuck out. The first one was a tall ass nigga. He looked like Tupac, especially with the way he had his blue bandana tied around his dome and the diamond studded nose piercing. The second man, who had hopped out on the front passenger seat, was a short nappy headed dude. He had a big bumpy nose and scruffy facial hair. His five foot five frame was in a blue Dickie suit two sizes too big.

"Sup? Low Life." the tall ass nigga greeted Killa Dre with a permanent scowl on his face. Low Life was the new leader of the Eastside Crips.

"'Sup wit it, my nigga? Killa Dre." he returned the greeting.

"I got word you wanted to holla at me."

"True dat."

"Speak on it." He gripped his wrists behind his back.

"This war we got going on, homie, it's bad for business."

"You ain't neva lied."

"It's hard for niggaz to eat with The Ones rolling back and forth through the turf, making shit hot and locking mothafuckaz up. You Griff me?"

"I feel you." The entire time the men kept eye contact. This was a non threatening way to test a niggaz manhood. Neither of them saw weakness in one another though. They were both Gs. "What do you propose?"

"Dead this beef so we can get back to getting this check."

"You talking 'bouta truce?"

"No doubt."

"So, what? You niggaz waving a white flag?" Gonzo butted in the conversation.

"Aw, naw, homeboy, we most definitely not waving no white flag," Banga stepped up into Gonzo's face, he was three inches taller than him, but it didn't matter because that little nigga wasn't backing down. He was as fearless as a mean ass pit bull. Both thugs nostrils pulsated and jaw muscles flexed.

"Banga, chill, blood!" Killa Dre called out to his homeboy.

Low Life stepped beside Gonzo and slithered his arm around his shoulders, speaking into his ear in a hushed tone.

"Be easy, G, let's hear the man out." he said to his homie and then looked to Killa Dre. "You got the floor."

Banga kept his eyes on Gonzo as he spat on the ground and then took a step back.

"Like I was saying," Killa Dre started back up again. "I think it's in our best interest that we let bygones be bygones."

"I hear you. I'm down with ceasing fire, but it's gotta be something in it for us?"

"Alright, you doing yo' thang over there on yo' part of town, right? You the man?"

"Something like that."

"What chu moving?"

"Same thang everybody else moving...crack."

"Some bullshit, ain't it?"

Low Life made a funny face and tilted his hand from side to side, signifying that the potency of his drugs was so, so.

"Well, check this out," Killa Dre began, taking the time to gather his thoughts before continuing. "You know what we were moving on our side? That shit that had both of our O.Gs beefing?"

Low Life nodded and said, "Yeah, I heard that shit y'all had on deck was some pretty superb shit."

"Straight up," Killa Dre nodded. "Look, if we can agree to this lil' treaty I'm willing to hit chu witta couple of them thangz for a nice price."

"Now we're talking, how nice though?"

Keeping his eyes on Low Life, Killa Dre told Banga to get him an ink pen from out of the Escalade. The hoodlum reached inside of the passenger side window and opened the glove box, removing an ink pen. Having closed the glove box shut, he pulled the upper half of his body out of the truck and handed his man the pen. Killa Dre wrote a number down on the palm of his hand and showed Low Life and Gonzo. Their eyes lit up and they nodded their heads approvingly, feeling the digits that they had been hit with.

"Alright, alright, alright," Low Life replied, letting him know that the quote he was given definitely had his approval.

"Bool," Killa Dre capped the ink pen and passed it back to Banga. "So, do we have a deal?"

"Them numbers are lovely, but you gone have to sweeten the pot just a tad bid."

"Man, fuck this negotiating shit! These some greedy motha…" Banga began but he was cut short when Killa Dre threw up his hand.

"You gotta excuse my homeboy, he's a hothead. Never mind him." Killa Dre took the time to clear his throat with his fist to his mouth. "Now, what were you saying?"

"Like I was saying, before I was so rudely interrupted," Low Life mad dogged Banga and looked to Killa Dre. "I'ma need something else to sweeten the pot."

"Like?"

"Well, we lost a hell of a lotta homies in this beef, and I feel it's only right that y'all offer up at least two of y'all homies."

"Nigga, you must be…" Banga started again but Killa Dre cut him short. He stepped into his face and spoke in a hushed tone.

"Blood, I got this, get in the truck."

"Man, these niggaz tryna…"

"Banga!"

Banga blew hot air and reluctantly climbed into the front passenger seat of the Escalade.

Once his homeboy got back into the truck, Killa Dre went back to chopping it up with that nigga Low Life.

"Lemmie get this straight," he flicked his nose and continued. "You want a deal on some birds and two of our homies and we got ourselves a truce?"

"That's right," Low Life nodded, "I want two of yo' niggaz. I want a man of your choosing and that nigga Booby."

"Booby?" Killa Dre's eyebrows rose and his eyes grew big. He couldn't believe his ears.

"Yeah, you heard right, I want Booby. Do we have ourselves a deal?" he extended his hand.

Killa Dre looked back through the windshield at Banga. He could tell by the expression on his face that he had heard the business proposition that was presented to him. He waited for his response and he shrugged. Turning back around to Low Life and his extended hand, Killa Dre shrugged.

"Fuck it. You got yo'self a deal," he shook Low Life's hand.

There was no such thing as loyalty.

That night

He sat on the couch in the dark, swirling the dark liquor around in his glass as he stared vacantly at the burning fire inside of the fireplace. His jeweled hand rubbed on the old wounds on his chest and torso, feeling the nasty looking lumps there. It was years ago that he'd received them, but he'd never forget the night that it all went down. He'd played the scene over and over again inside of his head. His face was already balled up with anger, and the more he thought about what had occurred, the tighter his face balled. He clenched his jaws and they pulsated like a beating heart, causing veins to etch up his temples.

The night after being shot he remembered being able to quickly get upon his feet from his adrenaline pumping so fast. He used this to his advantage and sprinted across the parking lot towards a woman who'd just opened the door of her Nissan Maxima. He snapped her neck with ease and ducked off inside of her vehicle, firing it up and pulling off. He drove himself into the emergency ward where they performed an emergency surgery to remove the bullets. He woke up sometime later to be questioned about being shot by detectives. Homie gave them a bullshit story that they didn't really buy, but what the fuck could they do?

It took a couple of years before he rehabilitated from his wounds. And as soon as healed up he was back on the streets doing his thang and chasing them dollars. But the streets were talking about the mothafucka that had put a few holes in him. Niggaz started to think he was soft for not exacting revenge. He knew he had to do something if he was going to keep being able to get money in The Concrete Jungle without some fool testing his gangsta every five minutes. So, with that in mind, he concocted a plan to get some get back for how he'd been done.

A golden orange illumination shone on his face from the flames of the fireplace as he took a casual sip of his alcohol beverage and swallowed. Hearing a knock at the door, he rose to his feet and made his way to the door, chrome .9mm in his jeweled hand. Shutting one eye, he peered through the peephole. Having seen who it was, he tucked his banger in the front of his slacks and unlocked the door. He pulled it open and a short big head nigga came waltzing in over the threshold, holding a manila envelope. After shutting the door behind him, he met his guest at the center of the living room.

"What chu got for me, Mookie?" he asked the little nigga.

"What you've been waiting for." Mookie smiled proudly, handing him the manila envelope.

He snatched the manila envelope from his clutches and opened it, pulling out several photographs. He was smiling until he started going through the photos. The smile slowly disappeared from his face the more photos he saw.

"This isn't him." he gritted.

"What? Gimmie that!" Mookie snatched the photos away and went through them. "What're you talking about? This is him. This the mothafucka you wanted dead." he looked at him like he'd lost his goddamn mind.

"It's his fucking brotha," he smacked the photos out of his hand and they went up into the air, raining down to the carpet. In a flash, he whipped out his burner and grabbed Mookie by his throat, pressing his heat into his left eye socket. "How did you manage to fuck this up? I gave you a specific name and description."

"I...I don't know, man. I guess they got the names and scripts mixed up." he spoke with terrified eyes, hands up trembling.

"Grrrrrrr." he mad dogged him, pressing his steel further into his eye socket and causing him to grimace. He held his gun there for a time before taking it down and shoving him backwards. Plopping down on the couch, he sat his strap down and poured up another glass of hard liquor. "Leave me."

"But..."

"If I rise from off this couch, you and I are gonna have a situation." He warned him.

Figuring that he'd better not try the nigga'z bluff, Mookie shut his mouth and left the house.

***

"Man, fuck these fools at?" Banga asked, impatiently drumming his fingers on the steering wheel and looking about. He, Pavielle and Killa Dre was chilling in the Escalade waiting for Fuller and his crew to pull up so that they could make the drop.

"Niggaz shoulda been here, on me." Killa Dre glanced at his watch.

"Be patient, homie will turn out." Pavielle assured him. He was wearing his hood on his head and the shadow it provided shaded half of his face, making only his mouth visible.

"I don't know, big homie, this shit could turn out to be a setup or some shit," Killa Dre reasoned. "Maybe we should fall back and see what happens."

"He's gotta point, ya know?" Banga addressed Pavielle. "How we know fa sho' dat dis dude took care of that business? Homie coulda got popped, and using you as leverage to make a deal, you feel me?"

"Y'all two niggaz are paranoid, man," Pavielle shook his head sadly. "Relax. Everything is everything. Watch. Just gotta give this mothafucka a lil' time."

Killa Dre took a deep breath and threw his head back, slumping down in the backseat. He folded his arms across his chest.

"If you say so, my nigga," Banga placed a half smoked blunt between his lips and punched in the truck's lighter, waiting for it to heat up.

"And I do say so, young nigga."

The whip was silent for a couple of minutes, and then Fuller came driving up. The headlights of his Chevy Trailblazer looking like two bright white orbs.

"I told yo' ass, now pop the trunk, pimp." Pavielle told Banga and hopped out of the car. The hoodlum did as he said, watching Fuller and the rest of the C.Os that were in on the jail hit hop out of his truck. They all wore serious ass expressions as they trekked in the direction of the Escalade. Killa Dre and Banga mad dogged them and gripped their heaters, but the men didn't pay them any mind.

"Yo, you think we shoulda flanked big homie?" Banga inquired from Killa Dre, still watching the men that had arrived.

"Nah, you heard what blood said, we just gone play our positions." Killa Dre replied, watching the men like a hawk.

Pavielle lifted the trunk and stood aside, motioning his hand towards the inside of the trunk. Inside there was five leather bowling bags. All of the men grabbed a bag except for Fuller. He slapped hands with Pavielle in greeting and then passed him a manila envelope. Afterwards, he grabbed his bag and slammed the trunk shut, turning to the man that had paid him handsomely to knock off the Mexican convicts back at the correctional facility. He watched as the man opened the manila envelope and pulled out the photos inside. While he was doing this, the other correctional officers were unzipping their bowling bags and peering inside at the money crammed inside.

Pavielle looked over the photos inside. They were of the Mexicans that he had called for to be knocked off. The eses were laid out at different angles with looks of horror etched on their faces. One was fried charcoal. Smiling with satisfaction, Pavielle put the photos back inside of the envelope, sealed it and set it on fire. He allowed the flames to devour half of the envelope before tossing it inside of a raggedy, rusted barrel.

"Almost forgot," Fuller reached inside of his back pocket and pulled out a folded slip of paper, handing it to Pavielle. "That's ol' boy's home address."

Pavielle smiled with satisfaction, looking the paper over. "Good looking out."

"We good?"

"Most definitely." he extended his hand.

"Cool." Fuller smirked and slapped hands with him, snapping his fingers.

With the officers paid off, Pavielle hopped back inside of the Escalade. He gave Banga the okay to start up the truck and leave. While he was doing this, he took something out of the glove box as he kept an eye on the rearview mirror.

Having seen the officers board the vehicle that they'd came to the meeting in. He gave Banga the signal to slow the whip to a crawl. The hoodlum did as he was ordered. Killa Dre and Pavielle stared out of the back window at the Chevy Trailblazer that the correctional officers were in. As soon as the last door of the vehicle had slammed shut, Pavielle pressed a button on the detonator he'd removed from out of the glove box. Instantly the ride exploded, sending burning wreckage and body parts flying everywhere.

Thunk!

A severed burning arm landed on the roof of the Escalade. Banga brought the truck to a screeching halt. Pavielle ordered Killa Dre out of the whip to remove the flaming limb. Hurriedly, the young nigga hopped out and pulled out his steel. He knocked the frying arm off of the truck with his gun and jumped back into the backseat, slamming the back door shut. With that, Pavielle settled back in his seat and motioned Banga to drive off. He then took the liberty to fire up a cigarette and blow out a gust of smoke. Cracking the window, he stared at the side-view mirror watching the burning wreckage and feeling accomplished.

    Murking out the correctional officers was a necessary evil. It had to be done in order to ensure that having the

Mexicans killed wouldn't come back to haunt him. The way he saw it, he couldn't gamble with his freedom. He didn't know them niggaz like that, and for all he knew they could have folded under questioning if it came down to it. Them crackas had a talent for breaking mothafuckaz, so letting those cats back there live was out of the question. Fuck that! A nigga had to do what he had to do to survive.

    Now, with that loose end tied up, Pavielle moved to take care of the other nigga that Chop had given him before he sent his bitch ass off to meet Satan. Pavielle reached inside of his pocket and pulled out the folded slip of paper. He studied the name and address that he had on it. After storing the information in his mental database, he used the ember end of his square to burn holes in it.

Chapter Nine

Later that night

Danz, dressed in his pajamas, made his way down the hall with a butt-cushion pillow in hand. He moved as careful as possible but was still wincing. Coming inside of the living room he found his television on TMZ. He sat his pillow down on the sofa and went to sit down.

Boom!

Splinters flew as the front door was kicked open. Three masked men rushed in with guns in hand, ready to give anything moving inside a flat-line. Danz eyes widened and his mouth formed an O. His entire body trembled all over and his knees buckled. He was scared as shit.

The tallest of the threesome sped walked over to him and cracked him in the jaw. He spun around like a fucking ballerina and hit the floor on a bending knee, holding on to the back of the sofa. His bottom lip dripped blood on the carpet and his head bobbled about, as he was in a daze. Pavielle kicked him in the head and he fell on the floor. Banga and Killa Dre watched as their big homie kicked and stomped the shit out of the old man, not giving a mad as fuck. Speckles of blood clung to the back of the sofa and nearby furniture.

Pavielle took his foot back having stomped Danz one final time. He stood over him breathing hard as hell, chest jumping up and down. His intimidating eyes studied his handiwork, proud of the brutality that he'd just laid down. He pulled his mask up so that his identity would be shown to his victim. Next, he whipped out his .9mm and *click clacked* one into the chamber. He pressed his cold steel to the old nigga'z temple as he attempted to get up from off the floor. The warden froze in the pose that he was in the middle of getting up in. His left eye was swollen shut and his nose had doubled in size, dripping blood. Parts of his face were bruised black and blue. He'd caught an ass whipping that he'd never forget.

"This is for my brotha, bitch," Pavielle went to pull the trigger.

"No! Wait, stop!" Danz held up a shivering hand. His head tilted to the side from the gun pressed against the side of it. The expression on his face told how terrified he was at the moment; that and the fact that he had a dark spot at the crotch of his pajama pants from pissing on himself. He was that afraid.

"Fuck a wait, nigga, my brotha waiting for you," Pavielle barked, then looked up at the ceiling. "Here comes anotha one, Gucci!"

"Please, I didn't have a choice!" Danz blurted out, hoping he wouldn't be murdered on the spot.

"Everybody's gotta choice and everybody's gotta die!" he hurled back. "And your time is now. Goodbye, mothafucka!"

"No," he threw up his other shivering hand. "You don't understand...they made me do it! They blackmailed me!"

"They blackmailed you? Who?" Pavielle's forehead wrinkled. Banga and Killa Dre exchanged glances. They were wondering just how deep this rabbit hole ran.

"Two men," he threw up two fingers. They were shaking so badly that they looked like he was holding up four fingers. "They kidnapped me and took me down into the basement of this abandoned house. They were...They were...Oh, my God...." he broke down sobbing and brought his wrinkled hands to his tear slicked face. He quivered as he cried. Figuring that he'd better start talking before he got his head blown off, he went on to tell Pavielle what he wanted to know. "They...They sodomized me and stuck their dicks...in my mouth." he broke down sobbing again, slobbering every fucking where. He wiped his snotty nose and wet cheeks with the sleeve of his pajama shirt.

"That's some bullshit, Danz," Pavielle shot back, shaking his head in disbelief. "Old nigga, you better start shooting me cold, hard facts 'fore I start popping off this cold, hard gat, you Griff me? Tell me something, pimping, 'fore I leave yo' thoughts on the ceiling."

"Everything that I have told you is the truth. I even have proof." Danz assured him, still shivering and sobbing.

"Well, where the fuck is it?" Pavielle spat. His gun was still pointed down at the old man and he was moving around like he was anxious and shit.

"It's in the sofa's cushion...The one on the right side end." he pointed with a crooked finger.

Pavielle gave Killa Dre the nod and he grabbed the cushion, unzipping it. Reaching inside, he pulled out a DVD in an emerald case. He opened it and slid it inside of the DVD player. Danz turned his face away from the screen seeing himself being fucked up his ass by a scrawny, smoked out looking nigga and mouth fucked by a stubby Asian man. The Asian man was holding a gun to his head as he jabbed his dick in and out of his mouth, saliva oozing out of his grill. Both rapists hooted and hollered like a couple of drunken white fraternity kids. The men sexually assaulting Danz were going for broke on him. His face was red and so were his ass cheeks, which had the scrawny nigga'z hand imprint on it from him smacking it.

Banga and Killa Dre looked away not wanting to see the disgusting sight.

"Turn that shit off, blood!" Pavielle ordered.

Killa Dre killed the show with the remote control.

"I'm sorry. I'm terribly sorry, but if I didn't do what they asked then they would have made it viral and humiliated me." he bowed his head to the carpet, wetting it up with his teardrops and slobber.

"Alright, tell me why these niggaz wanted my brotha touched."

"I...I don't know, I swear." he admitted, barely audible. "They just showed me his picture and told me to order the hit, or they would expose the footage to the masses."

"How do you get in touch with these fools? You gotta number or something?"

"Yes, yes, it's inside of my cell phone. I saved it under Ralph's supermarket." he went on to tell Pavielle where his cellular was and he sent Banga to go get it. Paville, still holding his banger on Danz, searched through the device until he found the number that he was looking for. Coming across it, he stashed the cell inside of his pocket and focused his attention back on the old man. He would use the GPS app inside of it to track down the fools that had raped Danz and bring their lives to an end.

"Look at me," Pavielle demanded but he wouldn't dare look up at him. "I said, 'look at me, goddamn it.'" Danz looked up at him, shivering and crying. "How much did you pay them May Mays to kill broski?"

"Broski?" his forehead creased. "What's...What's a broski?"

"My mothafucking brotha, nigga, who else!?" spit flew from off Pavielle's lips. His sudden outburst startled him.

"One...One...One hundred dollars each." he confessed, praying inside of his head that his answer didn't get him killed.

"Damn, six hunnit funky ass dollas, blood?" Banga hung his head and shook it shamefully.

"That ain't shit!" Killa Dre also shook his head shamefully.

After receiving his answer, Pavielle shut his eyelids and bit down hard on his bottom lip. When he peeled his eyelids back open, his eyes were glassy and tears came slicking down his cheeks hastily. He wiped his eyes with the back of his fist and gripped his weapon with both hands.

"Six hundred dollas, blood. My brotha's life was worth six Benjis to niggaz?" he shook his head, hating to hear that one of the people he loved most in the world life was worth so little to someone. "You got any last words 'fore I peel yo' scalp, nigga?"

"Please, I…"

"Please? I'll make sure it gets chiseled on yo' tombstone." his face twisted into a scowl and he squeezed off rapidly.

Boc! Boc! Boc! Boc! Boc!

He let all of that heat go in that mothafucka'z cap and lowered his smoking burner.

"Let's go." Pavielle motioned for his hittas to follow him as he headed for the door.

The next day

Pavielle pulled up to the Old Chinatown Center Plaza in downtown Los Angeles. He stole a glance through the rearview mirror to make sure that he hadn't been tailed. Seeing that the coast was clear, he hit the hazards, the AC and knocked on the dashboard. The stash spot shot out like the cash drawer of a register and he pulled out a lumpy black velvet sack. Drawing the strings, he opened the sack and peered inside: stacks and stacks of rubber-banded wrinkled dollar bills of all denominations were suffocating inside.

Pavielle drew the drawstrings closed and stuffed the sack inside of his jacket. Once he secured that thang on his waistline, he threw the door open and jumped out of the Regal. He dropped several quarters into the meter and went about his business. Stepping foot on plaza grounds, he zig zagged his way through people coming and going, as he moved towards his destination. Coming upon the establishment where he had business, he pushed open its door and the bell residing above it jingled. Chinese Folk music played softly in the background. He turned to the bronze life size statue of Buddha and rubbed its belly for luck. He had been doing business with the shop's owner for quite a few years and he'd done this every time he entered the store.

"Booby, welcome, my friend," a voice came from his rear, garnering his attention. He turned around to find an old stubby Chinese man. He had a balding scalp of white hair and matching beard. He filled out an ugly red Hawaiian shirt and Khakis. At the moment, he was sucking on the end of a black pipe with gold trimming, expelling weed smoke into the air.

The men smiled and greeted one another with an exclusive handshake and hug. After the pleasantries were exchanged, the old man brushed past Pavielle, in step towards the door. Pavielle stated his business as he watched the old man lock the door and turn the Open sign over to its *Closed* side.

"I need something that'll stop a nigga cold in his tracks, O.G."

"Hmmm," the old man's eyes looked to their corners as he stroked his beard, thinking for a time and puffing on his pipe. "Hunting big game, huh? How do you want this prey? Belly up or taking a nap?"

"Taking a nap," He told him. "I've got something specially planned for 'em."

The old man smiled sinisterly showcasing his beige crooked teeth and the blacken lips he'd inherited from smoking weed over a long period of time. "Yes. I have just the thing. Follow me." He strode towards the back of the store, motioning for Pavielle to follow with a chubby hand. The young kingpin followed the old man towards the back of the store, looking around at all of the items as he moved ahead. The store owner led him across the foyer to a thick, dull burgundy door. The door looked like it had seen better days with all of the nicks and chips in it.

"Hold on to this for a sec," he passed Pavielle his pipe. The old man reached into his pocket and produced a golden skeleton key, it gleamed under the lighting. He held the doorknob and stuck the key into the keyhole below, turning it. There was a click and the door popped open. He took his pipe back from Pavielle and held the door open for him to enter. He then stepped inside, closing the door shut behind him.

The storage room was small and cramped. There was about five feet of space to move about in. The storage was loaded with an assortment of merchandise, mostly illegal shit. There were boxes and crates stacked upon each other. Shotguns, assault rifles, machineguns, knives, daggers, grenades, bows and arrows, were just some of the things that were inside of the boxes and crates. The boxes and crates were stacked almost to the ceiling. At the center of all of the boxes and crates was a large pinewood chest with a padlock. The old man kneeled down to the chest and took the necklace containing the key to the chest from around his neck. He stuck the key into the padlock and turned it, opening it. He opened the chest and inside there was a smaller chest. He opened that chest, then the next, then the next, until he reached a case. He sat the case on top of the chest and opened it with the key. He lifted the lid of the tin-box and exposed what was inside.

Twelve metal tranquilizer darts containing a royal blue liquid were nestled in the velvet roof placement of the case. At the bottom of the case there was a matching tranquilizer gun. It shined under the soft light inside of the storage space

"May I?" Pavielle stopped in mid-reach of the tranquilizer gun. The old man nodded as he puffed on the pipe, polluting the air with smoke. The young kingpin picked up the tranquilizer gun. He licked his thumb and slicked the sighting at the end of the barrel. He then pointed the tranquilizer gun at a box at the far corner of the room, testing the sighting on the weapon. He sat the tranquilizer back into its space inside of the case and picked up one of the tranquilizers. He tossed the tranquilizer over in his hand as he addressed the old man.

"There isn't any poison in these things, is there?" he asked, continuously tossing the tranquilizer over in his palm.

The store owner shook his head and blew out smoke, saying, "No. No venom, just a very strong Chinese sedative. You may have to use more than one depending on his size. How big is this prey we're discussing?" he took a couple more puffs on the pipe, creating clouds of smoke.

"He ain't that big. In fact, he's a tall, skinny bastard." Pavielle told him.

"One should do the trick then. You remember my quote?"

"Yeah," Pavielle cracked a smile as he reached inside of his jacket and pulled out the sack. "A king's ransom, right?" he tossed the sack over to the old man and he caught it. He drew the drawstrings and peeked inside, smiling like a kid getting the gift he wanted for his birthday. Pavielle sat the tranquilizer back inside of the case and closed it shut. He picked it up by the handle and caught the key as the old man tossed it to him. He looped the necklace containing the key around his neck.

"Them Russian AKs you got on deck over there?" Pavielle spotted a barrel of assault rifles. They were all wearing red tape on them.

The store owner looked over his shoulder and spotted the weapons that he was referring to. "Yeah, but those fire blanks. They're movie props. Hell, I gotta couple of squibs, too."

"Squibs?" his brows furrowed.

"They're packed with blood. They're rigged to explode whenever the mechanism attached to them is triggered." He informed him. "I bought all of this shit some time back. I collect a lot of stuff from films. Those things were used in one of the first Rambo movies believe it or not."

"That's what's up." Pavielle nodded. "Anyway, nice doing business witchu, O.G."

"'Sho 'nough."

They exchanged pleasantries and the young kingpin made his departure.

***

Banga and Killa Dre sat in the Escalade truck in the parking lot of an apartment complex that was still under construction. Their heads were on a swivel looking for the niggaz that were supposed to meet them at that location.

"I know these fools betta show up soon, blood." Banga said, nodding his head to the sounds of Meek Mill's *Big Daddy,* "Got us out here waiting with this fucking cargo and shit."

"There they go." Killa Dre announced, seeing Low Life and Gonzo approaching through the rearview mirror in his SUV. Killa Dre nudged his partner in crime and they hopped out of the truck, making their way around to the rear of the enormous vehicle.

"Who you got for us, homeboy?" Low Life asked, wearing his signature scowl as he and Gonzo jumped out of his ride.

"Yeah, y'all niggaz have betta come correct." Gonzo looked from Killa Dre to Banga threateningly.

Banga clenched his jaws and mad dogged the shorter man. He clenched his fists so tight that veins bulged in them. He was about to make a move on him, when Killa Dre stretched his arm across his chest, stopping him in his tracks.

"Fallback, my nigga," Killa Dre spoke to his homie, but kept his eyes on the crips.

"Yeahhhhh, do what cho daddy says." Gonzo jokingly taunted him. This agitated Banga but he knew just how important this deal was for them so he obliged Killa Dre.

Banga and Gonzo stared one another down with their hands near the guns stashed on their waistlines. Getting stern looks from their respective comrades, they both decided to let that shit slide.

Seeing that everything was good, Killa Dre decided to go ahead and conduct the business at hand. He popped the hatch and lifted it up. Inside there was a nigga in a red T-shirt and a red bandana, tied around his head Tupac style. He was shaking he was so fucking scared. His eyes were red webbed and glassy from crying. He looked around at all of the gangstas surrounding him accusingly.

When Low Life saw the blood lying on his side in the hatch gagged and bound, he smiled devilishly and rubbed his hands together. He couldn't wait to torture his mothafucking ass.

"What's this fool's name?" Low Life asked.

"B.G. He's a new booty." Killa Dre told him.

"Awww, man, this a fresh fish?" Gonzo complained, looking disappointed. "I thought we 'pose to getta reputable."

"Nah, nah, nah," he shut his eyelids and shook his head. "Ya man said he wanted a nigga from our set, notta reputable nigga from the set."

"Hell naw, fuck…" Gonzo was cut short when Low Life grabbed him by his arm and turned him away from the earshot of Killa Dre and Banga.

"Chill the fuck out, nigga. The man's right." Low Life said through clenched jaws. "We said two of they homies. Now, cuz may be a nobody in our world, but that nigga Booby is most def' a big fish, ya feel me?"

Gonzo took a deep breath and massaged the bridge of his nose. "Alright, cuz, let's just get this nigga and go."

"Pop the trunk, loc." Low Life nudged his right hand man.

Gonzo popped the trunk of the old school Cutlass. He and Low Life grabbed B.G under his arms and made to take him to the open trunk. The Y.G struggled along trying to break free of their grips. Seeing that he was giving them trouble, Low Life whipped out his cannon and cracked him across his melon twice, knocking him unconscious. He went limp in their arms and they drug him the rest of the way, tossing his mothafucking ass into the trunk of the hood classic. They then slammed the trunk shut, smacking imaginary dirt from the palms of their hands.

"We good?" Killa Dre inquired.

"Nah, we'll be good once we get that nigga Booby and the work we agreed upon."

"I gotchu."

Low Life and Gonzo hopped into the Cutlass and pulled off. Killa Dre and Banga watched the back of the vehicle until its back lights disappeared into the darkness.

"Sucka ass niggaz," Banga shook his head shamefully. "Let's roll, blood."

The hoodlum and Killa Dre hopped into the Escalade and smashed out.

Banga and Killa Dre pulled the wool over the crips eyes. The nigga that they gave them didn't have any gang ties. In fact, his name wasn't even B.G. They made that shit up. His name actually was Devon Robertson. The poor bastard made the mistake of running his own operation outside of the organization. As soon as Killa Dre caught wind of this, he went looking for his monkey ass. When he and Banga caught up with him, they were just going to blast on him. But then they remembered the deal that they made with Low Life.

Flashback

Banga and Killa Dre stood over B.G with their guns pointed at him. He lay on the floor of his motel room asshole naked. His fuck-buddy cowered on the bed under the sheets, crying and hoping that the gangbangers didn't lay her down after they were finished with her trick for the night.

"Dat's yo' ass nigga," Banga bit down on his bottom lip and made to pull the trigger. The gun was just about to recoil from it being fired when Killa Dre grabbed him by his wrist. When he looked to him, he shook his head no. Banga lowered his burner to his side. "Alright, you don't wanna smoke this fool? Then what chu got planned for 'em?"

"That deal with Low Life," he answered. "Remember we gotta kick in Booby and anotha one of the homies."

"Yeah, and?" Banga raised his eyebrows.

"This fool could be that homie!" he pointed his gun at Devon. He was still lying naked and holding the side of his bleeding head.

Banga cracked a smile and massaged his chin, nodding. "Blood, you and that beautiful fucking mind of yours. I could kiss you."

"Nigga, you kiss me and I'll shoot chu," Killa Dre tucked his burner at the small of his back. "Come on, help me tied this nigga up and toss his ass into the trunk. I gotta foolproof plan."

After making Devon get dressed at gunpoint, Killa Dre restrained his wrists and gagged his mouth. He already fit the appearance of a thug with all of his tattoos and shit. So they fitted him with a red bandana and matching red T-shirt. He really looked like one of the homies now. Once they stashed him in the trunk, Killa Dre called up Low Life and told him that he had one of the bargaining chips in their agreement.

Present

Banga ripped down the street with the windows down in the Escalade, the cool air rushing in ruffling him and Killa Dre's clothing. He looked to his homeboy and cracked a mischievous smile, dapping him up.

"We got them ol' busta ass niggaz, dawg." Banga declared, grinning.

"Niggaz fell for the okey doke, blood." Killa Dre gave responded, lighting up the roach end of a blunt and blowing out smoke.

"Yo," he called for his comrade's attention. The expression on his face was a very serious one.

"'Sup?" Killa Dre threw his head back and took another pull from his bleezy.

"We really finna turn Booby over to these fools, man?" Banga looked back and forth between the windshield and his homeboy.

He thought on it for a minute and then looked back at him. "We don't have a choice."

Banga blew hot air and looked away, shaking his head pitifully. He didn't want to go through with what the homie had planned, but he was for what was best for the squad.

Sometime later

Devon aka B.G dangled from the ceiling by his rope bound wrists, head snapping from left to right looking for the men that had brought him down into the basement of the decrepit house. He was shivering all over. His forehead was shiny from sweat, snot oozed from his nose and tears accumulated in his eyes. He was so scared that he was going to cry again.

"Mmmmmm, mmmmm," he tried to say something but the gag in his mouth muffled him. Right then, he heard a drawstring being constantly yanked back until something that sounded like a lawnmower kicked twice, before eventually starting up. The noise was coming from somewhere within the shadows, but he couldn't quite put his finger on where. The area was pitch-black besides the light illuminating him from above.

Just then, Gonzo emerged from out of the shadows. He was wearing goggles and dressed in a black leather apron. His hands were covered in yellow dishwashing gloves and holding tight to a chainsaw. Its blade was shiny and running so fast that it was blurry. He smiled evilly as he brought the chainsaw to B.G. The poor bastard thrashed around wildly on the rope. His eyes were big and frightened, terror gripping his heart like a pair of strong hands.

Low Life played the sidelines, taking casual pulls from a blunt. He watched attentively as his homeboy pressed the chainsaw's blade into their hostage, splattering his face and body with blood. B.G danced on the end of the rope with a face masked by excruciating pain. Suddenly, he stopped moving and went limp on the rope. Gonzo brought the chainsaw down to his side and stared up at the mess of dangling, bloody flesh that he had created.

Chapter Ten

That night

Jerome stood at the center of the living room punishing the worn out Everlast punching bag that dangled from the ceiling. He was a tall bug eyed nigga that had skin the color of onyx. He was so scrawny that the bones in his chest and ribs were visible. As of now he was in a du-rag with the flap and jeans two sizes too big, which he kept upon his waist with a rope. Jerome was high as a kite right now. For some strange reason he liked to get stoned and relive his glory days as a Golden Gloves Boxer. He had big dreams back then. But after a couple of mafia goons broke his hands and legs for failing to throw a match, chasing his habit replaced all of the goals that he set for himself. Nowadays, the thirty-five year old crackhead spent his days chasing a dollar so he could afford his poison of choice.

"Unh! Unh! Unh!" Jerome attacked the bag with a finesse that hadn't been seen since he was inside of the ring, causing the chain that held the bag to rattle. His face and body was covered in beads of sweat. Sweat that flew from off his form with each calculated punch that he threw, making the Everlast bag dance.

"Get 'em, Rome! Get 'em! Fuck 'em up! Fuck 'em up!" This was Stu. He laughed and displayed his mouth of missing teeth, clapping his hand on his thigh. He was amused seeing his partner in crime attack the punching bag like he had a beef with it. He was just about to fire up the glass stem in his calloused hand, when all of Jerome's punching grabbed his attention.

Having seen enough of his right-hand man's shenanigans, Stu sat back on the tattered black leather couch holding the flame of his lighter to the end of a glass stem that housed off white crack rocks. His dry, cracked fingers held tight to the stem while his face balled up like he had a stomach ache. The smoking utensil scorched black from the flame of his lighter, causing the drugs to crackle and pop. Once the smoke manifested inside of the glass dick, he took a strong pull and drew the intoxicating vapors inside of his lungs. After one long pull, he took another, then another, and another. Having gotten enough, he took his ashy thin lips away from the stem and allowed a fog to roll off of his tongue. He fell back on the couch, slumped with a crooked smile across his lips, obviously enjoying his high.

Stu was a short, big head, Asian nigga that wore his hair in a bowl cut. He had a wide nose and craters in his cheeks. At the moment, he was dressed in a yellow tank top that had twin dragons facing the opposite directions of one another on it. The jeans he was sporting were dingy and torn at the knees. His flat crusty feet were inside of sandals, displaying his yellowing toenails.

Before him sat a flat wooden board that was propped up by two blue milk crates. Upon it were two freezer Ziploc bags of small bags of crack. Lying beside it was a few wrinkled hundred dollar bills. This was the money that they were given to rape Warden Danz and record it. The job was easier than they thought it would be and they came back ten stacks richer. For the last few days the two old chums had been kicking up their feet and relaxing, enjoying the fruits of their labor.

"Unh," Jerome punched the bag one last time and dropped his arms at his sides, breathing hard. His bird chest rose and fell with each breath that he took in through his lungs. "Fuck this shit, man." he marched over to Stu and took the glass stem and lighter from out of his hands, firing it up himself.

"Mannnnn, we been getting fucked the fuck up allllll muddafuckin' week, my nigga," Stu busted up laughing and sat up on the couch.

Jerome took the time to blow smoke out into the air before replying. "Yeah, this shit is lovely, my nigga. We made off with a pretty big bag from that move we made. I mean, I ain't like fucking dude up his ass 'cause I ain't no faggot, but I'd do the shit again if it meant anotha payday like this. You feel me?"

"I feel you," he nodded in agreement. "I ain't gay either, but if it meant getting paid like this here again," he scooped up a handful of the wrinkled dead presidents and fanned them before his face, smiling and boasted his missing front teeth.

"See, me and you, my chinky eyed friend," he moved two fingers between them. "We're on the same page. I made it so we ain't gotta steal, jack or pawn notta mu'fucking thang else."

"Oh, yeah? How is that?" Stu asked, eying the money as he counted it up.

"You know that footage of the rape I gave the old man and told 'em that it was the only copy? Well, that wasn't the only copy. I kept a copy of it."

"Get the fuck outta here." Stu looked up at Jerome with big eyes and a big ass smile. He was surprised because he truly believed that his homeboy had given the old geezer the only copy of the DVD.

"Yep, so you know what that means, right? We gone bleed that honky dry."

Together, while slapping hands, they said in unison, "Mo' money, mo' money, mo' money!"

"Youa genius!" he jabbed his finger at Jerome.

"I be knowing."

"Gimmie some, man." he held out his hand.

Jerome slapped hands with Stu and bumped shoulders with him.

Boom!

The door rattled from a brute force and stole their attention. They looked to it with furrowed brows, wondering what the fuck was going on. The force impacted the door once again and it came open, sending a chunk of the door's frame spinning across the room. Stu went to grab his gun from off the couch that he'd sat there before getting high. Before he could lift that bitch all of the way up his chest exploded with a massive hole, causing him to grimace. His little five foot ass flew backwards and slammed into the wall, knocking a large hole in it.

Jerome looked from his homie to the masked nigga with the gun. He wanted to take off but he was terrified of taking some hot shit in his back.

Seeing that his skinny ass was thinking about running, Killa Dre aimed his long, chrome shotgun at him. His demeanor behind the trigger told the crackhead that if he made a move that he was going to find himself lying dead beside his homeboy. Jerome shut his eyes for a moment and swallowed the lump of nervousness in his throat.

"Move and I'ma flip yo' ass like a quarter bird!" he grumbled angrily, slowly moving in on the crackhead. He pulled some zip-cuffs from his back pocket as he moved to restrain him. But hearing a moan of pain stole his attention. His head snapped to the right and he found Stu moaning in agony, moving his head from side to side, his eyelids narrowed into slits. Seeing that the gunman was occupied with his dying comrade, Jerome kicked his foot up in the air. His oversized sneaker went spinning through the air, looking like an off white blur. It hit its intended target in the face and he fired his shotgun at the floor. With the gunman temporarily blinded, Jerome took off running as fast as he could, foot in one sneaker. He lifted up the window and climbed out of it, jumping down into the backyard. He took off, running as fast as his body would allow him, occasionally looking over his shoulder. His eyes were wide and his mouth was open, seeing the gunman climbing through the window. Homeboy was coming after his ass and he was determined to get him by any means necessary.

"Unh!" Jerome hopped a fence and took off down the block, hearing barking dogs as he cleared a nearby house. "Haa! Haa! Haa! Haa! Haa!" his body oozed with sweat as he ran, chest warming from his burning lungs. Although he was scared, he wasn't about to stop. Fuck no, he wanted to live another day to smoke crack.

Suddenly, he felt something prick the back of his neck and he slowed to a trot. Stopping, he pulled a tranquilizer dart from the back of his neck. He looked at it and frowned, dropping it to the sidewalk. He felt another prick at his back and he grimaced. He pulled a tranquilizer out of his back and dropped it. He was seeing double now and feeling funny all over. He took off running, but felt sluggish. Still running and looking down, he noticed that he was barely moving. Hearing someone running up behind him, he whipped around and found someone with a red bandana over the lower half of their face. His gloved hands gripped a tranquilizer gun and it was aimed straight at him.

"I give up!" Jerome spoke slowly and threw his sluggish arms into the air, surrendering.

The man wearing the red bandana over the lower half of his face, eyebrows arched and he curled his finger around the trigger. The gun slightly recoiled when it unleashed a tranquilizer dart. The dart stuck to Jerome's forehead like a refrigerator magnet and he went cock eyed. His entire body went into paralysis, like he'd been poisoned by the venom of a snake. He fell to the sidewalk, busting the back of his dome. His head fell off to the side and everything went black.

The man walked up on an unconscious Jerome with his tranquilizer gun trained on him. He kicked him to make sure that he was out for the count. Seeing that he was, he holstered his weapon and pulled out some zip-cuffs. He turned him on his stomach and cuffed his hands at the rear of him. By the time he was done doing this, he heard a large vehicle coming to a screeching halt beside him in the streets. He looked up and saw Banga behind the wheel.

"You got Killa?" Pavielle, who was wearing the red bandana on the lower half of his face, asked. Killa Dre leaned forward in the front passenger seat and held up his chrome shotgun. His ski-mask sat on top of his head like a beanie. He was wearing a serious face when he gave him an assuring nod.

Pavielle took in his surroundings to make sure no one was watching him before hoisting Jerome over his shoulders. The skinny crackhead farted as he was carried off and Pavielle frowned, turning his face away from the foul stench. He knocked on the hatch and Banga popped it open. Once Pavielle lifted the hatch, he deposited the man he'd been looking for into the back of the SUV and shut it. Quickly, he hurried around to the back door of the truck and climbed inside, slamming the door shut behind him. With that mission completed, the black beast sped off the block.

An hour later

"Rahhhhhhhhhhh!"

His eyes and mouth were stretched so far that they hurt his face. His eyes were red webbed and running with tears. Veins pulsated at his temples, neck and arms. His wrists and ankles were wrapped in chains. One end of him was secure to a tree while the other was secured to the back of the Escalade truck, Banga behind the wheel mashing on the gas.

"Aaaaaaah!"

The flesh of his arms and legs began tearing, dripping blood, having been stretched beyond its limits. He was screaming so loud that he was starting to become hoarse and his head was killing him. He had a fucking migraine, but he couldn't tell the vindictive man what he wanted to know. That was a big no, no. If the nigga that had hired him ever found out then he would torture his ass, too. Probably far much worse, but he couldn't think about that now. Hell, how could he? His mind was consumed with pain. So what some nigga could be doing to him now didn't even matter.

"Stop!" Pavielle called out to Banga, keeping his eyes on the poor bastard hanging in midair before him. Once the Escalade stopped, he hung there moaning in excruciation. His eyes were rolled to the back of his head and blood was trickling from his wounds. He was in bad shape. I mean, really bad shape.

Pavielle and Killa Dre stood side by side, observing Jerome as he bled out. There was silence as they listened to him, his white breath shown in the cool night's air.

"You ready to tell me what I wanna know, homie? Huh?" his maddening eyes staring down at him. He didn't feel any pity for the sorry mothafucka before him. As far as he was concerned, he may as well have been one of the Mexicans that had butchered his brother. "You hear me talking to yo' funky ass? Huh?" he kicked the shit out of Jerome in his ribs, causing him to howl in agony. The crackhead was sure that his captor had broken at least two of his ribs. He could feel his side throbbing, so he was sure that he was bruised, too.

"I can't tell you, man! I can't tell you 'cause he gone kill me!" Jerome hollered out, whining like he was born with a pair of tits and a big ass.

"He gone kill you?" Pavielle's face tightened with anger and he clenched his jaws. "You worried about that mothafucka? You needa be worried about this mothafucka standing, right here?" he smacked his hand up against his chest heatedly. "Now, start talking for they need two coffins to bury yo' ol' busta ass in!"

"I can't, man! If I do, he'll…." he was cut short when Pavielle called out to Banga to speed up the truck. The chains clinged as they straightened and his bones crackled, stretching. "Ahhhhhhhhhh!"

"Stop!" Pavielle called out again, eyes still on that nigga Jerome.

"No more...no more, unh," The crackhead said out of it. His entire body was exhausted from all of the stress it was put under being pulled from both ends.

Pavielle leaned closer to Jerome and smacked him so he'd be looking at him. His head turned to him, but he could still tell that he was barely conscious.

"You ready to sing now, lil' birdie?" he asked. Jerome nodded his compliance.

Pavielle turned his ear towards his victim's lips. His eyes widen as he listened to what he was being told. The man's name he was given was thought to have been dead, but as it turned out he was sadly mistaken. He was indeed alive.

Having recorded the name of the man behind his brother's murder and the address where he could find him, Pavielle went through the crackhead's jeans until he found his cellular. He had been told that this was the cell that the shot-caller had given to him to keep in contact until the arrangement was taken care of.

Pavielle flipped open the cellular and looked through the contacts. There was only one name there. Seeing this, he flipped the device closed and stashed it inside of his pocket.

"Can...Can I go?" Jerome asked almost pleadingly.

"Yeah...to hell," Pavielle looked to Banga. "Mash that mothafucka, blood!"

Vroooooooooom!

"Ahhhhhhhhhh!"

Jerome hollered aloud, his voice echoing throughout the woods.

The speedometer's hand spun all the way around to the other end and dust kicked up in the air, as the Escalade lurched forward. Pavielle stared down at the man as he hung there, screaming in antagonizing pain. He smiled wickedly as his suffering seemed to bring him great pleasure. The tortured man's shrills was so excruciating that Killa Dre stuck his fingers in his ears and scrunched up his face.

"Aaaaah!" Jerome's voice raised several octaves. The flesh of his torso stretched and blood oozed out of it, blood pelting the dirt. The center of him stretched so far that his spine cracked and he eventually snapped in half. His bloody intestines, stomach, spleen and some other sick looking shit hit the ground, rolling in the dirt. The upper half of Jerome went up high into the air. His face still held the mold of him screaming in agony as it finally crashed to the ground. Next, the lower half of him hit the surface and his legs lay twisted at awkward angles. The Escalade skidded to a stop and idled, its exhaust pipes unleashing smoke.

Pavielle stood there for a time admiring the bloody mess that lay before him, his eyes studying it like he had plans on what else he was going to do with it. In the night the only thing that could be heard was the exhaust pipes of the Escalade and its driver side door closing shut. Banga had jumped out of the black beast and came to stand alongside his homeboys. They all stared down at the mess that was once Jerome the mothafucking crackhead.

Pavielle threw his head back and stared up into the sky, "You see how yo' lil' bro giving it up, Gucci? You see how I'm putting the smash down on all of these bitch ass niggaz that had anything to do witcho murder? I got one mo' and then you can finally rest in peace. On bloods." tears rolled down his cheeks and he threw up two B's, the universal gang sign that stood for Bloods. He hung his head and allowed his hands to keep the signs up. He was having a moment of silence and so was his hittas. Banga and Killa Dre stood on either side of him. Their heads were hung and they held their wrists at their waists.

At the end of the night vengeance would be Booby Loco's.

Chapter Eleven

"Yeah, well, these niggaz here I'm talking about can fuck up a cup of coffee," the man spoke heatedly into his burnout cellular phone. He was perched on the living room couch breaking down Kush buds. "The wrong fuckin' one, playa, I gave them niggaz there the 'script and eh thang. I don't know how they managed to fuck that up." He shook his head and scowled, he couldn't believe the Mexicans hit the wrong fucking Hood Brother. "Anyway, I need you to get up with that cat you were telling me about. You know, ol' boy that be laying his thang down? Damn, what's his name?" he winced and snapped his fingers trying to recall the hit-man's name, mulling it over and over again in his mental database. "The Ghost, that's it. What's his prices like? Damn, a hunnit of them guys? Fuck it. It will be well worth it. Yeah, main, gone set that up, I got the whole thang faded. Smooth. Peace."

He disconnected the call. Afterwards, he began sprinkling the weed throughout his blunt and licked it closed. He laughed in between doing this, as he was watching The Honey Mooners on the living room television set.

"Bahahahaha, that Fred is a fool, boy." He observed the happenings on the TV as he picked up a Bic lighter, sweeping its flame back and forth underneath his blunt to seal it shut. Once he was done, he tossed the lighter back upon the table top and took a couple puffs of his bleezy, expelling smoke into the air. "Hahahahahahaha!" he smacked the table's top as he laughed hysterically. Hearing his Doberman pinscher barking in the backyard, he muted the television with his remote control and mashed out the bleezy. Grabbing his chrome .9mm from off the coffee table, he rose up from the couch and cautiously approached the kitchen, listening closely. Suddenly, he heard the dog yelp and things became deathly quiet. He stood where he was for a time, waiting to hear something, and then, the backdoor rattled from a powerful impact. The blow splintered some of the frame and startled him. He brought his ratchet up, gripping it with both hands and pulling the trigger. It kicked twice as it unleashed on the backdoor.

He kept his eyes and his weapon on the door. Everything was perfectly still and quiet. Thinking he'd killed whoever was on the otherside, he slowly moved in on the door. Big mistake!

Boom!

The door flew open from the second impact and sent splinteres flying everywhere. Pavielle, wearing a red bandana over the lower half of his face, let his .9mm join the party.

Boc!

The man howled in pain and dropped his ratchet to the floor.

"Pavielle!" he gasped, eyes growing as wide as saucers. The color drained from his face and he looked like he was about to have a mothafucking heart attack.

"I'm here to finish what you started..." he glared at him with threatening eyes and twisted lips. He let that thang off again, but by this time homeboy was on the move.

Boc! Boc! Boc!

Some hot shit flew over his head. Holding his shoulder, the man went running across the living room as fast as he could. His sights were set on the large window. This would be his salvation. With a grunt, he leaped into the air and dove through the glass, shattering it. His body came through on the other side followed by shards. He hit the front lawn and rolled forward, falling on his chest. Grimacing, he pushed up off the surface. His face and hands were covered with small red cuts. When he peeled his eyelids open he found a dark figure in what appeared to be a hood. It held something long at its side, dangling. It suddenly moved forward and stopped before him. Slowly, it pulled its hood from off its head, revealing its identity and its head of sandy brown cornrows. It was Vayda, and she was wearing a menacing scowl.

"Yo...yo...you," the man stammered. His eyes were big and his mouth was wide open. The mothafucka looked like he'd seen a ghost.

Vayda hoisted up her shotgun and racked it, just as Pavielle stepped outside onto the porch. He jumped down on the front lawn, moving in his intended target's direction, gun at his side. The man stole a look over his shoulder, but quickly looked back around into the unforgiving eyes of the Creole beauty. She'd just aimed her shotgun at his bitch ass and was about ready to let it rip. Petrified, the fuck-nigga raised his trembling hands into the air and stood erect. His entire form trembled like he was naked and it was 30 below outside. At his front and back were some straight up head bustas and they wanted blood...his blood.

"You remember me?" she asked.

"Yeah...yeah," Buddy answered.

Flashback

Buddy scrambled to his feet, his jeweled hand clutching a straight razor. His hairy chest jumped up and down as he breathed heavily, cheeks huffing and puffing. His usually curly hair was a mess. There was a swelling under his right eye and his silk blue shirt was torn. He wiped his swollen bleeding lip with the back of his fist and swallowed the blood that had filled his grill. It tasted of metal but he didn't acknowledge it. Nah, his attention was solely focused on Vayda who was crawling away from him. Her eyes were set on her handbag which had her nickel plated .22 hanging halfway out of it.

"Fuck you think you goin' bitch? I ain't done witcho mothafuckin' ass yet, not by a long shot." he swore, his lethal eyes held firmly on her as he stalked after her, taking his sweet time. "I'ma carve you up like a Christmas goose." He licked his chops and bit down on his bottom lip.

Tears flooded Vayda's swollen face, mixing in with the blood running from her nose. She moved as fast as she could with a twisted ankle, trying to make it to her handbag where she knew her piece was. Buddy had given it to her in case some trick overstepped his boundaries and she had to set him straight. Now she had every intention of using it on his ass if she was able to get her hands on it.

Vayda had just grabbed her handbag and gripped the small gun, when she saw Buddy's shadow eclipse her on the carpet. Her eyes widened with fear and she gasped. His grunting flooded her ears and she felt fire rip back and forth across her back. Through the floor she saw his shadow swinging a straight razor back and forth across her back causing her to grimace, narrowing her eyelids into slits. She shrieked in excruciation and tried to reach over her shoulder instinctively to stop him, but he started slashing at her hand as well, opening up a nasty gash on it.

Vayda howled in pain and looked at her ruined hand, oozing with bright red blood. Her mind was quickly taken away from the pain though, because he continued to hack away at her rear, making it look like bleeding pastrami meat. "Arghhhhh!" Tears flushed down her cheeks and she bit down hard on her bottom lip to combat the excruciation from the blazing fire in her back. Gripping the small gun with both hands, she turned around on her back and pointed the deadly end of her weapon at her attacker's chest. He froze where he stood, with his head tilted down, chin resting in his chest. His eyebrows were lowered and he was glaring down at her, lips peeled back into a sneer. His shoulders rose and fell as he breathed, blood droplets falling from the end of his blade, soiling the carpet.

"Now, just what in the fuck do you plan on doing with that, huh? Yo' lil' red ass ain't built for no mur..." Pow! *A shot to his chest cut his shit talking short. His eyes widen with surprise and his mouth hung open. He touched the hole in his chest and his palm came away crimson. He couldn't believe it. That bitch had really shot him.* "You...you...you fuckin' whore!" *he roared and his eyes darkened with hatred. Screaming in a rage, he charged at her with his razor held above his head ready slice her down to the bone. Squeezing her eyelids shut tightly, Vayda pulled back on the trigger of her weapon. It kicked back when it spat back to back, propelling him backwards with every bullet released. Pow! Pow! Pow! Pow! Buddy dropped his straight razor as he went staggering back getting tangled up in the curtains and went crashing through the window's glass. He hollered out as he went hurtling towards the apartment complex's parking lot. Still clutching her gun and wincing, Vayda slowly scrambled to her feet, clenching her jaws to combat the sharp pains zipping back and forth across her back. She crept towards the window with precaution and placed her back up against the side of it. Carefully, she looked over and out of the window. A surprised expression went across her face when she only saw broken glass and the curtains below.*

Present

Buddy swallowed his fear of dying and looked Vayda dead in her fucking eyes. His plan was to hurt Vayda to the core of her soul by taking out the love of her life, Pavielle, but the hittas he sent fucked that up royally. After she was left grieving such a tragedy, he'd move in and deliver the kill-shot to her. He wanted her to be miserable as fuck before he brought her to her death. Scowling and gritting his teeth, Buddy's jaws throbbed. He harped up some phlegm and spat off to the side.

"Well, what the fuck y'all waiting on?"

Bloom! Bloom! Bloom!

Vayda's eyelids narrowed and she clenched her jaws, squeezing the trigger of her powerful weapon. The roars of it spun Buddy around to Pavielle and he lifted his heat, letting that thang spit that hot fire at his punk ass.

Boc! Boc! Boc! Boc!

Vayda let her shotgun join in on the firefight alongside his tool, letting her ex-pimp catch it from both sides. For a time he stood on his feet taking all of that heat until both parties weapons registered empty and he fell face first to the ground. He lay with the side of his face mashed against the lawn, his wide eyes staring off at nothing. The smell of gunsmoke and blood lingered in the air. Vayda and Pavielle stood where they were, studying their handiwork, their chests rising and falling rapidly. Their husky breathing could be heard in the night along with police car sirens. The couple lowered their weapons at the exact same time. Pavielle interlocked his fingers with his woman and they ran out of the yard, looking both ways. Seeing that the coast was clear, they fled off into the night taking the sin that they'd committed that night along with them.

An hour later

Banga pulled up three houses down and executed the engine of the G-ride. He and Killa Dre were up front while Low Life and Gonzo played the backseat. They were masked up and clutching AK-47s.

"This the spot?" Low Life asked, trying to look to the side of Killa Dre to see the house that they were casing.

"Yeah, this is it." Killa Dre assured him.

"Cuz, you sho?" Gonzo asked, trying to get a look as well.

Killa Dre's face balled up and he replied, "This the spot...*Blood*. Now, all we gotta do is hit this nigga up so he can come out."

Banga hung his head and shook it shamefully. Killa Dre looked to him and felt like the biggest piece of shit in the world for what he was about to do.

"You alright, Banga?" he asked concerned.

"This shit foul. This shit real foul, Killa." He looked at his nigga and he could tell from the look on his face that he didn't really want to let him go through with it, but he couldn't turn back now. It was far too late. The wheels had already been set to turn, and once they stopped everything would change. He would be running the empire that Pavielle left behind and making an elephant's shit load of money, especially once the war was over. He didn't want to give up the position of That Nigga in the Streets for loyalty. Hell nah, fuck that! Niggaz had their turn and now he wanted his.

"It's too late to turn back now, Banga. I just needa know you gone ride this thang out with me before I go ahead with it." He looked his right-hand man dead in the eyes as he held his cellular in his hand. Pavielle's number was on display and he was ready to call him to come outside. If Banga said he wasn't gonna go along for the ride then he was going to nod that ass right there and right now. He didn't need to have to worry about him gunning after him later. So he figured he may as well get him out the way now. This is why his banger was in the pocket of his hoodie, but aimed straight up at Banga's forehead. It was so dark inside of the car that the hoodlum couldn't even see it. At the distance that Killa Dre was sitting, he'd have to be blind to miss him.

Complete silence passed between the two gangstas. Banga's heart pounded inside of his chest and his decision went back and forth across his mind like a ping pong ball. He weighed his decision carefully before he made up his mind. What he decided was going to change the rest of his life as he knew it. So he had to be wise with his decision.

"I'ma ride witchu 'til the wheels fall off, Blood. You know my pedigree, I'ma G 'til I close my eyes foreva." he pounded the Blood B against his chest.

"That's what I'm talking about." Killa Dre hit up Pavielle and told him to come outside. After he flipped the cell shut, Low Life and Gonzo jumped out of the G-ride.

***

After successfully laying down Buddy's bitch ass, Pavielle and Vayda got rid of the murder weapons and dipped back home. They gave Tay, Mad Man and the other two niggaz that were holding them down the go ahead to leave while they packed their belongings to leave Killa Cali. They stored all of their stuff inside of their luggage and went about the task of packing little Nasheed's stuff up. As Vayda was packing the baby's diaper bag, Pavielle's cell phone went off. He ignored it and went about his business of helping put away his son's things, but its constant ringing begged for his attention.

"Bae, you should go ahead and answer that. It could be Killa or Banga." Vayda reasoned.

"Yeah, you're probably right," Pavielle stopped what he was in the middle of doing and pulled out his cellular. Killa's name was on the display. "'Sup wit it?" he said into the cellular, his eyes wandering around the room as he listened to what he was being told. "Okay. I'll be right out."

"Who is that?" Vayda asked, keeping her eyes on the task at hand.

"The homie, I'll be right back." he stashed his cell in his pocket and left the bedroom, heading for the front door.

***

Hurriedly, Low Life and Gonzo moved in on the house. Pavielle had just come out of the house and made his way towards the fence. His eyes lit up when he saw those two masked up niggaz run up on him, AK-47s raised to spit that hot fire.

Killa Dre and Banga shut their eyelids. Their bodies jumped having been startled from the sounds of automatic gunfire. Tears ran down both of their faces. They listened to the heavy breathing of the crips and their hurried footsteps, as they hauled ass back to the G-ride. With their heads hung, at the exact same time, they crossed themselves in the sign of the crucifix. As soon as they finished they heard the backdoors of the vehicle open and slam shut, quickly. Low Life and Gonzo pulled their ski-masks back up from their faces.

Low Life smacked the back of the driver side headrest hastily. "Pull off, nigga! Pull off!"

Banga fired up the engine and mashed the fuck up out of there.

An hour later

After discarding the weapons, clothes and torching the G-ride, Banga and them hopped into a silver Challenger that they'd rented out. He dipped out to Low Life and Gonzo's hood to drop them off. They both hopped out of the whip. Gonzo went into the house, but Low Life fell back to kick it to Killa Dre for a time.

"Yo, good looking out on that business." Low Life told him.

"Don't mention it." Killa Dre replied. "You just make sure you keep your end of the bargain."

"Don't wet it. I'ma call a meeting tomorrow and tell the homies that we gotta truce. It may be hard to swallow at first, but once they find out that we got some A1 product on deck it'll smooth things over. You feel me?"

"Two sho'," Killa Dre nodded. "But check it, I'ma pick that up tomorrow. You just make sure you got that for me."

The young nigga was speaking on the money for the product that he was buying off of him to put his entire hood back in the drug game.

"What time, my nigga?" Low Life inquired.

"I'ma hit chu up."

"Alright, that's what's up," he took his hand out of his pocket and dapped him up. Afterwards, he looked both ways and jogged across the street, disappearing inside of the house that Gonzo went in.

"Where to now?" Banga asked Killa Dre.

He opened his mouth to respond, but his cellular's ringing stopped him. When he pulled it out of his pocket and seen Vayda on the screen, he already knew what time it was. It was showtime.

"This that nigga'z Booby's wife right here now." he informed the hoodlum.

"What chu about do?" lines creased Banga's forehead.

"Give her an Oscar worthy performance," Killa Dre cleared his throat with his fist to his mouth. He then pressed answer and brought his cell phone to his ear. "'Sup wit it, V? What? Awww, naw, not my nigga." he sat up, listening to her go crazy over the phone having come outside to see the love of her life had been murdered in coldblood. "Where y'all at? Bool, I'ma pick up that nigga Banga and I'ma meet chu at the house then. Alright, twenty minutes." he disconnected the call and looked to his right-hand man. "You ready?" he asked, wondering if he was ready to encounter a distraught Vayda.

"As ready as I'm ever gonna be, my nigga." Banga shook his head and threw the Challenger in drive, smashing out. They were headed to the house out in Compton to play the roles of the concerned homeboys and scream promises of revenge.

With friends like these, who needs enemies?

Chapter Twelve

Pavielle's funeral fell on a gloomy Sunday afternoon. Some of everybody came out to pay their respects to the fallen kingpin. Bloods, crips, eses, Asians, wise guys. He had dealings with them all in some way. They all saluted his gangsta and admired the way that he did business. Whether you loved or hated the young man you had to admit that he was one standup guy. He was honorable and stuck to the code of the streets.

There was weeping and crying during the ceremony's proceedings. A long line of people approached the polished black wood coffin that Pavielle was lying face up in, placing items inside: red bandana, bankrolls of money, brass knuckles, a knife, a gun, pictures, jewelry, etc. The women would kiss him on his cold lifeless cheek, but the homies would say a few words or bang the hood one last time.

Creeper, Bullet and Black Jesus came out to show their love and support for Pavielle's family and friends. In fact, the South American drug lord footed the bill for the entire funeral service and dropped a hefty bag in Vayda's lap. Vayda seemed to be taking everything pretty well. That was until she found herself staring at her husband inside of the coffin. The realization finally set in that her man was gone and he wasn't ever coming back. Quickly, her eyes flooded with tears that threatened to drip over their lids. Her face twitched and she mumbled something encoherently.

A shrill at the center of the aisle seemed to steal everyone's attention all at once.

"Noooooo! Not my man, not my husband, not my king, God!" Vayda wailed aloud, tears cascading down her cheeks. Her manicured hands shook uncontrollably and she planted them on the sides of her head. She was frantic and heartbroken. Suddenly, she dropped to her knees and some of the niggaz there grabbed her by her arms, her legs were like cooked spaghetti noodles under her. She would have hit the floor had it not been for the homies there having a firm hold on her. "Jesus, Lord, why him, Father? Why take my man? Why my child's daddy? Why break up my family? Haven't we suffered enough, huh?" she stared up at the ceiling talking to The Almighty. The people in attendance looked on feeling sorry for her. Men and women wore tear streaked faces. It was like they could feel her pain. Her heartfelt cries sent chills down their spines and their condolences went out to her.

Abruptly, she went limp in all of the limbs that were holding her up. Her head dropped and she hung there, held in several arms. She cried and cried, big teardrops falling and hitting the burgundy carpet. Her entire body shuddered as she sobbed. From a far Killa Dre held Little Nasheed as he stared at Vayda, having witnessed her performance. His face was soaked with tears. He occasionally patted his tearing eyes with the red handkerchief from his suit's pocket, while cradling his God son in one arm. Banga stood off to the side of him, holding his wrists at his waist and staring ahead. His eyes had built up with moisture, but he quickly squeezed his eyelids shut to dissipate the tears.

"Damn, Booby, fuck, blood," he shook his head shamefully. The hoodlum was in an all black suit, with a red tie and red Hush Puppies. Now more than ever he regretted his decision to go ahead with Killa Dre's plan to set his big homie up. If he could turn back the hands of time he would in a heartbeat. But that was out of the question now. He had to live with his decision, just like Killa Dre did.

Banga looked to Killa Dre and saw that he'd been crying. He'd known Pavielle longer than him so they were closer. It was because of this that he could understand his pain. His tear drenched face made him wonder if he was regretting going along with the ambush as well.

"I fucked up, homie. I fucked up real bad," Killa Dre said to him in a hushed tone. "I shoulda never sold the homie out."

"It is what it is now. We made our beds and now we gotta lay in them." Banga told him, staring him square in his eyes.

Killa Dre nodded and said, "True dat."

Killa Dre and Banga dapped one another up. Turning their attention ahead, they watched as the niggaz that had caught Vayda before she fell helped her to one of the pews. After she'd settled down, the line kept moving with people bidding their final farewells to Pavielle.

"Fuuuuuck, man," Killa Dre dropped his head and shut his eyelids for a time. He then threw his head back and looked up at the ceiling of the church. "I'm sorry, Booby. I'm so sorry. I hope you forgive me."

Killa Dre and Banga focused their attention back up front, watching Vayda being fanned by two older women in big flower hats. They could tell by her movements that she was still sobbing. Her hollering could barely be made out over the cries of the organs.

"Oh my God! Oh, oh, oh my God," Vayda cried out.

Seeing her reaction caused Killa Dre to shed more tears and for Banga to finally release his own. Swiftly, he crossed his heart in the sign of the crucifix and silently asked God to forgive him for the role he played in his homeboy's murder.

Miami, Florida

Three years later

Vayda sat at the dining room table with little Nasheed in her lap and a photo album before them on the table top. They both smiled as she turned the pages of the photo album, looking at all of the pictures presented inside. Turning the last page, Vayda landed on a photo of their entire family. Stopping there, she and her baby boy studied the faces of the people on the photo. Suddenly, her eyes became hot and tears accumulated.

"Mommy, who are all of these people?" Little Nasheed asked his mother. He was so adorable with his natural grey eyes and dark curly hair.

"Well," she coughed with her fist to her mouth. She cleared her throat of her overwhelming emotions and tried to force back her tears. "All of these are your uncles. There's Woo, Big Head, Debo, Rhyda Man, Bully, Panic, Gangsta..." her emotions got the best of her and she broke down sobbing, tears falling down her beautiful face in buckets. "Gouch and your daddy, baby."

"Don't cry, mommy, it's gonna be okay." Nasheed wiped her face with his small hands and kissed her lovingly.

"I know, baby. Everything is gonna be just fine." she mustered up a halfhearted smile and wiped her tearing face with the sleeve of her shirt.

"We still have daddy." the little guy told her.

"That's right, son. You still have daddy," Pavielle hugged his wife and son from behind, kissing them both on their heads. Vayda turned him to her by his chin and kissed him hard and passionately. Using his thumb, he swept the tears from her cheeks and kissed her again. The trio then embraced as a whole.

Pavielle had faked his entire death with the help of Killa Dre and Banga. They pulled his coat to them taking the deal with the Eastside Crips. The young kingpin figured that they could use the situation to their advantage. The AK-47s that Killa Dre gave Low Life and Gonzo to murk him with were actually the weapons that fired blanks that he'd bought from the old Chinese man back at the shop. The kingpin had also copped the squibs used on movie sets. These were blood packs and would explode as soon as a mechanism was triggered. As soon as Low Life and Gonzo started popping off, Pavielle triggered the device that made the blood packs explode. In faking his death, he brought an end to the war and set Killa Dre up to be Top Dawg. Now he and his family could live peacefully without worrying about the law or any enemies coming back for revenge.

Los Angeles, California

Killa Dre sat in the barber's chair getting his hairline and goatee edged up. He'd gotten his dreads braided into plats, and was getting his hair on the sides tapered as well. At the moment, he was listening to Maddy and Cisero tell him and Banga about their run in with a couple of knuckleheads at the Santa Monica Pier. Ever since Killa Dre took over Pavielle's empire his life had changed for the better. He grew in money, power and status. He carried himself with the air of a boss and the attitude of a movie star. The nigga was breaded and he made sure his squad was, too. Their motto was "Everybody Eats" and the young nigga made sure of that shit. Because the last thing he needed was a nigga hating on him and putting salt in the game. He couldn't have that shit. Hell naw, he was trying to have longevity in the game and be rich forever.

"Alright, my man,"Mervin, his barber said, removing the smock from around him. He brushed the hair off Killa Dre and wiped his edges with green alcohol. Once he was done, he held a mirror out before his face so that he could get a good look at himself. Killa Dre gave himself the once over and flapped the loose hair from off his shirt. "We good, fam?"

"Oh, yeah, most definitely," Killa Dre rose from off the chair and dipped his jeweled hand inside of his pocket, pulling out a wad of bills. He peeled off two Benjamin Franklin's and passed it to the nigga that had cut his hair. He thanked him and stashed the rest of the money inside of his pocket.

"My man," Mervin motioned for Banga to sit down in the chair. He threw the smock on him and prepared him for a haircut, turning on the clippers. While he was doing this, Killa Dre was looking himself over in the mirror that stretched from one end of the wall to the other, his icey gold crucifix and 'Dre' chains clinking off one another. This was due to his movements; he was getting himself a thorough examination to see how his barber had hooked him up.

"Man, get cho ol' pretty boy ass outta the mirror," Cisero balled up the McDonald's cheeseburger wrapper and threw it at his homeboy; it deflected off the mirror and hit the floor, slightly tumbling.

"Fuck you, ol' hating ass nigga!" Killa Dre whipped around, giving his homeboy the middle finger.

"What chu doing ova there? Modeling and shit?" Mervin questioned, giving Banga an edge up.

"Blood, this nigga stay in the mirror," Cisero spoke again.

"You ain't neva lied, my nigga Killa be feeling himself." Maddy took a sip of her shake and lay back in the chair.

"You just hating 'cause you an ugly nigga, Blood." Killa Dre pulled his Levi's 501 jeans upon his ass; they were lying over some black Nike ACG boots, with the purple bottoms.

"Nigga, please, I got mo' bitches than you," Cisero declared.

"You betta stop lying like that for yo' nose grow, Pinocchio," Killa Dre chuckled, but stopped once he heard his cellular go off. He grabbed it and held up a finger as Cisero was still talking shit to him. A smile was on his lips as he placed the cell phone to his ear and made his way for the exit, pushing the door open. His narrowed his eyelids from the illumination of the bright sun shining on his face.

"'Sup, big homie?" Killa Dre smiled happily. "Man, I thought I'd never hear from yo' ass again. I miss the hell outta…"

Blowl!

The first gunshot went off, echoing throughout the area. The side of Killa Dre's head burst like a rotten tomato and he fell off to the side, lying awkwardly with his eyes as wide as saucers. The side of his face was pressed against the hot concrete. The blood running from his head wound was forming a puddle and outlining his dome. The warm rays of the sun beat down on his back.

Lil' Dontai lowered the ruined brown paper bag that his smoking gun was concealed in slowly, observing his victim. His young eyes didn't have any remorse after what he had done. He had claimed the life of the man that had murdered his father and now he felt that he could rest in peace.

Flashback

Reboc sat before a 42 inch flat-screen playing Fight Night on PS4 with Lil' Dontai. The scrawny, brown skinned kid was beating the living shit out of his ass, but the gang banging veteran didn't care. He had gotten a text earlier from Nike that said he was sending a car to get him to bring him back to the hood. Nightmare had his hands full with the war back home and he needed every able body he could get.

Drama was right up Reboc's alley, he had been cooped up in Nightmare's sister's apartment for the last couple of weeks. He had been confined there so long that he started to feel institutionalized, but he had to suffer through it. He was advised by Nightmare to lay low after he had caught a body. He was reluctant to do so, but when that crazy mothafucka advises you to do something you had better do it.

Reboc was excited. He couldn't wait to get back home and be in the mix of all the bullshit. So he didn't mind getting his ass handed to him by a seven year old.

"Boom! Boom! Boom!" Lil' Dontai said as his character delivered a three punch combination that laid Reboc's character on his back. He hopped up from the couch and counted the numbers the referee shouted as they appeared on the screen. "One, two, three, four, five..." Reboc rose to his feet punching the buttons furiously, trying to get his character back on his feet. The countdown continued on the screen with Lil' Dontai calling them out loud. "Six, seven, eight, nine..." Reboc clenched his jaws as he rapidly punched the buttons, desperately trying to make his character get back up on its feet. "Ten!" Lil' Dontai shouted, spiking his controller like a football. He jumped in Reboc's face talking a big shit. The Eastside Crip balled up in the corner of the couch laughing his ass off.

"Dontai!" a voice yelled from the doorway of one of the bedrooms. "Boy, get off Reboc, have you lost your mind?"

Big Dontai entered the living room taking pulls from a Sess blunt. He walked over to the couch and plopped down beside his son. Big Dontai was a reputable Blood from Black P Stones, who went by the name Tay-Rock. It was because of him that Reboc got to stay within The Junglez without some knucklehead putting heat to him.

"What's up, my nigga?" Big Dontai asked Reboc.

"What up?" Reboc responded.

"I see junior in here tapping that ass in Fight Night," Big Dontai ruffled his son's head.

"Yep, I was kicking his butt." His mini me chimed in.

"Yeah, lil' dude got me, but I'll get 'em next time, though." Reboc gave him a half hearted smile. He wasn't too fond of Big Dontai. To him he wasn't a man. All he did was eat, sleep, and shit while Nightmare's sister worked, took care of home, and their son. The nigga was a bum to the tenth power, but that wasn't any of his business though. He was just there to lay low until things blew over. So he was going to keep his mouth shut.

Big Dontai took a few more pulls of his blunt and then blew the smoke into the air. The smoke made his son gag and fan the smoke away.

"Wanna hit this?" Big Donai asked Reboc as he held out the blunt.

Reboc frowned at the stench of the burning blunt held out before him. "Fuck is that shit?" he asked disgusted, face balled up.

"Sess, my nigga; shit bomb." He replied, holding the smoke in his lungs.

Reboc looked at him as if he had just offered him a blowjob. "Man, I don't fuck with that shit, its Kush or nothing."

"More for me," Big Dontai shrugged his shoulders and continued to smoke his blunt.

Boom!

A spray of debris and splinters flew everywhere as the front door was blown open by a powerful kick. Two men rushed inside wearing ski-masks and clutching pistol grip pumps. Reboc dropped the PS4 controller and threw his hands up in the air, while Lil' Dontai cowered at the corner of the couch. Dontai jumped to his feet and darted towards the bedroom to retrieve his banger. He got about four feet before a blast spun him back around and a second slammed him up against the wall, decorating it with a crimson splatter. He slid down to the floor, slumped with his head hung and his palms up.

"Daddyyyyyyyy," Lil' Dontai screamed as he ran towards his father, tears spilling from the corners of his eyes. Before he could reach his father, the tallest of the ski-masked men grabbed him from behind and clamped his gloved hand over his mouth. Lil' Dontai flailed his scrawny arms trying to break free, but he was no match for the strength of a grown ass man.

When Reboc saw Dontai go down he closed his eyes and shook his head. He peeled his eyes open to find himself being eclipsed by the shadow of the shorter of the ski-masked men. Reboc put up the meanest mug he could muster and then looked up into the shorter man's eyes. He already knew that he wouldn't be living past that night, so he decided he was going to go out like the beast the streets claimed him to be. He harped up some phlegm and spat it on the shorter man's sneaker and smiled wickedly.

The shorter masked man looked from the yellowish goo on his sneaker to the wicked smile on Reboc's face. He pressed his pistol grip pump into his brother's murderer's palm. Before Reboc could snatch his hand away half of it was being blown off, blood and mutilated fingers shot across the living room. All that was left of Reboc's hand was a bloody thumb and stump. His eyes bulged and his mouth stretched open as far as it could as he screamed at the top of his lungs. He tucked what was left of his hand under his armpit and fell off the couch and onto the floor, bawling in agony.

"I bet chu see now what all that rah rah shit get chu, huh?" The short masked man kneeled down to a grimacing Reboc. He pulled the ski-mask off and Reboc looked into his face. He ran his face through his mental database but couldn't find a name to match it. He hadn't a clue as to who he was.

"Yo, Blood, what the fuck are you doing?" the tallest of the masked men asked. This was Gouch. He was still holding a squirming Lil'Dontai.

Killa Dre threw up a hand, calling for his homeboy's silence.

"That kid you shot down in the street as if he were nothing was my big brother, Tramel Johnson." Killa Dre spoke behind bloodshot eyes as tears slicked his cheeks wet. His talking was cool and calm, yet displayed the hurt and anger in his heart.

"So, fuck that nigga, you think I care?" Reboc hollered back into Killa Dre's face, spit flying from off his lips.

"Nope, but here's something you may care about," Killa Dre began, "Your lil' brotha Dizzy, Nightmare murked 'em. Why? Die wondering, mothafucka." He pressed the pump under Reboc's chin and pulled the trigger. Killa Dre shut his eyes just as blood smacked against his face. He rose to his feet wiping his face with the sleeve of his shirt. He kneeled down to the little nigga and motioned for his partner to release him. Lil' Dontai mad dogged Killa Dre as tears cascaded down his cheeks. He was so angry that Killa Dre could feel the heat radiating from him. The little boy wanted to kill him, but fear of being murdered before he could get revenge stayed his hand.

"Sorry about cha daddy lying over there," Killa Dre threw his head towards Big Dontai's dead body, "I'll chalk up his murder as a necessary evil. Being as how he was a loved one I'm sure his death has left you in your feelings. So when you grow up...if you still feel some type of way about it...I want chu to come see me. We'll settle up then."

Killa Dre and Gouch walked towards the door. They'd just about crossed the threshold when Lil' Dontai spoke.

"When I get bigger, I'ma find you and I'ma smoke your ass." Tears streamed down the little nigga'z face and his nostrils flared, standing there tight lipped.

Present

Hearing police cars hurriedly approaching, Lil' Dontai turned around on his Huffy and peddled off as fast as he could. He pulled his hood over his head and tucked the hand that was still inside of the mangled brown paper bag under his hoodie, keeping a close eye out for any witnesses that may have seen him. He sped off down the block, hearing police sirens growing louder and louder at his back.

"Killa! Killa! Killaaa! Killaaaa!" Pavielle blared over the cellular.

Damn, all a young nigga wanted to do was be the man. I mean, a real shotta, get money type of nigga, you Griff me? I wanted to make enough paypa to take me and my mom's out the hood, and I did that. But fuck, I wish I woulda stopped while I was ahead. These hands done touched a couple of mill in sucha short time. I gotta admit though, shit was lovely while I was out here doing my thug thizzle. But like the old saying goes, all good things must come to an end. Now, I knew that one day that I'd probably have to handle lil' dude, but neva, eva in a million years did I expect for him to come back so soon, and blasting too. I guess the G's are getting younga and younga every day, huh? Well, we all get our chance to shine, and then it's our turn to go. That's just how it is, my nigga. Well, at least while I was here we were doing it big, just me and my hittas.

    Killa Dre lay where he was bleeding in the gutter. Mervin, Cisero, Maddy and Banga, who was still wearing a smock, came rushing out. Maddy and Mervin kneeled down to attend to Killa Dre. Banga and Cisero stood where they were with their guns at their sides, looking up and down the block for the nigga that shot their homeboy.

    "Killa, get up! You've gotta get it, blood!" Maddy cried as she shook him violently.

    "Fuck," Mervin said, seeing he'd taken one to the dome. "Somebody call an ambulance!"

    "Killa, Killaaa, Killaaaaa!" Pavielle continued to blare over the cellular.

THE END

COMING SOON BY TRANAY ADAMS
The Devil Wears Timbs 6: Just Like Daddy
A Hood Nigga's Blues
Bloody Knuckles
Billy Bad Ass

A Tranay Adams Novel

AVAILABLE NOW BY TRANAY ADAMS
Me and My Hittas 1-6
The Devil Wears Timbs 1-5
The Last Real Nigga Alive 1-3
Fangeance
Bury Me A G 1-3
Tyson's Treasure 1-2
Treasure's Pain
A South Central Love Affair
Fearless

Me and My Hittas 6

A Tranay Adams Novel

www.ingramcontent.com/pod-product-compliance
Lightning Source LLC
LaVergne TN
LVHW021809060526
838201LV00058B/3297